Women
Reworked

Empowering

Women in

Employment

Transition

Heather Resnick

ISBN 1-894439-26-0
Printed and bound in Canada

For more information, contact Heather Resnick at hrighter@rogers.com. Telephone 905-889-4669, Toll-free 1-800-687-2169, fax 905-731-5189. www.womenreworked.com.

Production by Creative Bound International Inc.
Book design by Wendelina O'Keefe

Author photograph by As It Happens Photography Inc.

Library and Archives Canada Cataloguing in Publcation

Resnick, Heather
    Women reworked : empowering women in employment transition / Heather Resnick.

Includes bibliographical references and index.
ISBN 1-894439-26-0

1. Women--Employment re-entry. 2. Vocational guidance for women.
3. Women--Employment re-entry--Case studies. I. Title.
HD6053.R47 2006   650.14'082   C2005-907285-7

In Praise of *Women Reworked*

"Heather takes every opportunity to observe, to learn, to listen, and to contribute. She turned her experience into her book *Women Reworked,* a valuable tool for women who want to be re-employed."

Brenda Faktor, Facilitator, Breakthrough Program,
Academy of Learning

"Heather has achieved her life-long goal as a writer with her book *Women Reworked.* Her journey will inspire other women to follow their dream career."

Michèle Le Fèvre, Marketing Communications Manager,
Information Builders

"Heather is a keen observer of women's issues, specifically preparation to enter or re-enter the work force. She has channeled her life experiences and passion into creating her dream career of writing. Her book project *Women Reworked* is her commitment to empowering women to overcome their barriers in joining the labour force."

Marla Jameson, Employment Coach,
Focus and Learning Connections Programs

"Heather has a clear, concise vision in her book *Women Reworked.* She is a positive role model for women wanting to be re-employed."

Fatema Rashid, Mayfair Webmasters

"Heather's personal knowledge and drive have made her a compassionate advocate in her upcoming book, *Women Reworked,* for all women who want to re-enter the workplace."

Rosy Theeuwen, Financing and Marketing Manager,
Focus Program, York Region Learning Connections

"Heather's excitement about her book project *Women Reworked* is infectious. Her positive attitude and steely determination can only lead to success."

Rischa, Folk Artist

"Heather's compassion and personal knowledge of women re-entering the workforce, make her the ideal person to write *Women Reworked*."

Fern Lutwack, Teacher/Homemaker

"Heather is a funny, enthusiastic woman who will add value to women wanting to be re-employed with her book *Women Reworked*."

Leila Peltosaari, Author of Dancing With Fear

I lovingly dedicate this
book to my parents,
who worked hard for me to
have all the things that
everyone else had.

Disclaimer

Advice given in this book is for information purposes only. Please seek professional help if you require it.

This book is non-denominational. Any stories noting religious, cultural or political preferences belong solely to the contributor of that story and do not necessarily represent the view of the author, Heather Resnick.

Most of the information and services found in this book are external sources, not connected with the author, Heather Resnick. She is not responsible for the accuracy, reliability or currency of the information or services. Readers wishing to rely upon this information or these services should consult directly with the appropriate source.

Every effort has been made to ensure that the resources referenced in this book are accurate. If you find an error, please contact Heather Resnick at hrighter@rogers.com, so that this information may be corrected in future editions of this book.

Contents

Acknowledgments

My appreciation begins with those closest to my heart: My parents for always believing in me and giving me a lifetime of support. My siblings for being my cheerleaders. My dear children who have let me experience life from all sides. My deepest gratitude goes to my husband who has always been the rock of stability and who is the "wind beneath my wings."

A book of this nature is a collaborative effort. Thanks to the women of the Focus Program and the facilitators who gave me the impetus to start this project. A special thank you to the incredible women who poured their hearts out to me and honored me to write their stories. To the women who allowed me to quote their profound thoughts. To all of the women who responded to my on-line survey or answered my plea for stories. It was difficult to choose—everyone has an important story to tell. I apologize if I could not include all of your stories and thoughts. *Women Reworked* will have regular revisions with more stories to inspire and empower women to transition in employment. Your stories are always welcome.

My sincere appreciation to all the people from whom I solicited advice, who supported me and who helped me get the word out about this book or connected me with contacts:

Shelley Arch, The Regional Municipality of York,
   http://www.region.york.on.ca/Default.htm e-mail info@york.ca

Gail Baird, President, and Wendy O'Keefe, Creative Director,
Creative Bound International Inc.
http://www.creativebound.com/ e-mail info@creativebound.com
Murray Barrett, Senior Sales Manager, Picadilly Fashions,
http://www.picadillyfashions.com/home.html
Kay Blair, Executive Director, MicroSkills
http://www.microskills.ca/
Sandra Campbell, Publisher
http://www.womencandoanything.com/
Canada's Top 100 Employers 2004, Book, Mediacorp Canada Inc.
http://www.canadastop100.com/ e-mail ct100@mediacorp2.com
Ken Chapman, Account Executive, Kromar Printing
http://www.kromar.com/
Sheri Cohen former Executive Director of Alder (Adult Learning
Disabilities Employment Resources)
Jill Crossland, Life Coach, Publisher, *TimeFinders* on-line newsletter
http://www.timefinderscoaching.net/
e-mail jill@timefinderscoaching.net
Brenda Faktor, Breakthrough Facilitator, Academy of Learning
http://www.academyoflearning.com/
e-mail aolrichmondhill1@rogers.com
Phyllis Flatt, Community Fundraiser
Jacqueline Foley, Author, *Flex Appeal*, Out of Our Mind Press
http://www.getflexappeal.com/
e-mail Jacqueline@getflexappeal.com
Eleanor Getzler Community Development Officer, Richmond Hill
Service Canada Centre http://www.servicecanada.gc.ca/
Barb Gormley, former Editor *Active Woman Canada* magazine
Dr. Judy Goss, Ph.D, Sport Psychology Consultant 'Act Now'
http://www.actnowonline.ca/index.php

Anne Graham, Branch Manager Kelly Services (Canada) Limited
http://www.kellyservices.ca/eprise/main/web/ca/services/en/index.html

Barbara Florio Graham, Book Publishing Consultant
http://www.simonteakettle.com/

Patricia Holtzman, Seneca Richmond Hill Business Centre
http://www.senecac.on.ca/rhbc/

Marla Jameson, Employment Coach, Focus and Learning
Connections Programs, York Region Learning Connections
http://www.employmentsource.ca/

Joy Jensen, Director of Communications, Women in Community
Service (WICS) http://www.wics.org/

Miriam Katan, Dental Assistant

Carol Kleiman, Syndicated Business Columnist, *Chicago Tribune*
http://www.chicagotribune.com/

Diane Kriger, Ph.D., Editor kriger@sympatico.ca

Isabella Krikunov, Communications Branch, Human Resources
Skills Development, Canada (HRSDC)
http://www.hrsdc.gc.ca/en/home.shtml e-mail
ontario.inquiry@hrsdc-rhdcc.gc.ca

Elizabeth Kuzmas, Investment Advisor, BMO Nesbitt Burns

Frances Lankin, President and CEO of United Way of Greater
Toronto http://www.unitedwaytoronto.com/

Grace Laui, proprietor, The Aqua Shop,
http://www.gotoaquashop.com

Heidy Lawrance, Creative Production Services
http://www.hlacreative.com/ e-mail heidy@hlacreative.com

Linda Leatherdale, Financial Editor, *Toronto Sun*
http://www.torontosun.com/

Michèle LeFèvre Information Builders, Marketing Communications
Manager http://www.informationbuilders.com/

Fern Lutwack, Graphic Artist, Decorator

Shirley Marshall, Training Manager Survival Skills for Women
http://www.focustoledo.com/SurvivalWomen.htm

William McCutcheon, Accountant w.f.mccutcheon2@on.aibn.com

Diane McGee, Founder Women in Networking Growing Strong
(W.I.N.G.S.) http://www.wingscanada.com/ e-mail
headoffice@wingscanada.com

Laura Mealiea, Senior Director, Communications & Technology,
Women Work! The National Network for Women's Employment
http://www.womenwork.org

Donna Messer, President, ConnectUs Communications Canada
http://www.connectuscanada.com/
e-mail info@connectuscanada.com

Aisla Mulla, Toronto Area Economist, Human Resources Skills
Development Canada (HRSDC)
http://www.hrsdc.gc.ca/en/home.shtml
e-mail ontario.inquiry@hrsdc-rhdcc.gc.ca

David Murray, Knebel Waters & Associates, Career Transition
Management http://www.knebelwatters.com/

Andréa Nielson, Photographer, As It Happens Photography Inc.
http://www.asithappensphoto.com/
e-mail andrea@asithappensphoto.com

Peggy Phifer, Co-founder, Editor, *The Wordsmith Shoppe*
http://www.wordsmithshoppe.com

Leila Peltosaari, Author, *Dancing With Fear*
http://www.tikkabooks.com/ e-mail Leila@tikkabooks.com

Dan Poynter, Owner, Author, Para Publishing http://ParaPub.com,
e-mail DanPoynter@ParaPublishing.com

Wendy Preskow, Unit Leader, Creative Memories
http://www.creativememories.com/wendypreskow

Fatima Rashid, Web Designer http://www.mayfairweb.com
  e-mail webmasters@mayfairweb.com

Michelle Reid, Adult Support Group, Toronto Learning Disabilities
  Association http://www.ldatd.on.ca e-mail admin@ldatd.on.ca

Debbie Ross, President Women's Travel Network
  http://www.womenstravelnetwork.ca/
  e-mail info@womenstravelnetwork.ca

Royal Printing Printers http://www.royalprinting.ca,
  e-mail infor@royalprinting.ca

Dawn Rosenberg McKay http://careerplanning.about.com/
  e-mail careerplanning.guide@sbout.com

Rischa Sidon, Folk Artist

Francine Silverman, Author, *Book Marketing From A-Z*;
  Publisher/Editor, The Book Promotion Newsletter
  http://www.bookpromotionnewsletter.com/

Dr. Rhona Singer, Ph.D, Educator, Writer, Artist
  http://www.stonewomanwarrior.ca/
  e-mail rhonasinger@rogers.com

Manisha Solomon, President, Solotext Editorial
  http://www.solotext.com/

Brian Stephenson, Co-author, *Job Search Bootcamp*
  http://www.jobsearchbootcamp.com/

GraceTaller, Author, *Get Hired on Demand*, Creative Management
  Training http://www.newcomersupplies.com/
  e-mail order@newcomersuppies.com

Rosy Theeuwen, Finance and Marketing Manager, Focus Workshop
  for Women, York Region Learning Connections
  http://www.employmentsource.ca/

Nancy Toran Harbin, Executive Director, F.A.C.E. (Family Abuse
  Crisis Exchange) and Dress for Success http://www.face1.org/
  e-mail info@face1.org

Eke Van Der Zee, Individual and Relationship Therapist
eke@sympatico.ca

Cynthia Vella-Zarb, Eary Childhood Educatior

Diane Wagner, Resource Counselor, Learning Disabilities
Association Ontario http://ldao.ca/

Hazel Webb, Director, Community Programs, Community
MicroSkills Development Centre http://www.microskills.ca/
e-mail admin@microskills.ca

Karen Webb, Board Member, Community MicroSkills
Development Centre http://www.microskills.ca/
e-mail admin@microskills.ca

Renate Weiler, Motivational Speaker, Author, *Get a Grip*
http://www.renateweiler.com/ e- mail info@renateweiler.com

Cora Whittingon, Coach, Facilitator, Golden Pathways
http://www.goldenpathways.ca/ e-mail cw@goldenpathways.ca

Shelley Whyte, The National Women in Business Expo
http://www.nationalwomeninbusinessexpo.com/
e-mail info@nationalwomeninbusinessexpo.com

Christine Williams, Host and Producer, "On the Line," CTSTV
http://www.ctstv.com/fall

Loraine Woon, Service Delivery Co-ordinator, Human Resource
Centre, Human Resources Skills Development Canada
(HRSDC) http://www.hrsdc.gc.ca/en/home.shtml
e-mail ontario.inquiry@hrsdc-rhdcc.gc.ca

Sharon Yarmolinsky, Financial Services Representative
http://www.tdcanadatrust.com

YourNameSells.com, http:// www.yournamesells.com

A warm thank you to family members and friends who have shared
my journey with me and made me feel that my project was valuable.
Please accept my apologies if I have forgotten anybody.

Foreword

Two years ago, I began a quest of self-discovery. In the process, I found my voice as a writer. I also found the voices of other women who were lost or tormented by their pasts and were moved to seek fulfillment and their life's purpose or to follow their dream career.

I cannot begin to express the gratitude and respect I have for the women who expanded my world with their wisdom, their experiences, their zest for life, and their tenderness for the world around them. Some of those women had suffered great emotional and physical pain, yet still find humor daily.

In allowing me into their lives to write their compelling stories, they made me realize something important that all journalists should heed when they are writing about other people. As a writer, I am interpreting someone else's story. It is my job to make the words evoke feelings that will bring the reader into the realm of the other person's story. In other words, it has to be interesting for someone to read. However, I cannot forget that I am merely the messenger—the person telling someone else's story. Most of these women had never seen their stories in print.

Suddenly to have revealed their innermost feelings and fears, to name other people or companies who have no way to defend themselves or who could cause harm to the women, was sometimes overwhelming to them.

It was incumbent upon me to seek their approval for what I wrote.

Wanting to be respectful of their needs, I assured them that facts would be reported accurately and that any material that was offensive or caused them discomfort would be removed. Some of the women gave me great leeway to include portions of their lives that others would not consider for public consumption. Sometimes, though they had been anonymous their whole lives, they felt it was time to reveal to the world what it is like to be on the bottom, and how they struggled and fought successfully to rise to the top.

Not all the stories have deep, dark undertones. Some are light-hearted. What *is* common is that all of the women in my book want other women to know that you can succeed—no matter what your life may have been previously—with hard work, a belief in yourself, the help of others who want to see you thrive, and the ability to learn and grow. I am eternally grateful that they have entered my life. I have learned much from these women warriors. It is my wish that all of you will too.

Life is either a daring adventure or nothing.
Helen Keller

Chapter 1

A Life Fulfilled
Heather Resnick's Story

I was like many young women in the late 1960s: post-secondary education meant getting an M.R.S. While the feminist movement loomed, the extent of my compliance was not to burn my bra but to take it off after leaving the house in the morning, so my mom wouldn't be any the wiser. It was all about getting the man and living happily ever after.

Sure, I had a dream to be a journalist. When I stopped flirting, skipping classes, smoking and daring to drink wine in the washroom, or sneaking off for the odd adventure at the racetrack, I took my dream seriously. I was accepted into a Journalism Program at college. However, underlying that end was the desire to find a husband who would care for me and, of course, financially support me. I was naïve.

My ambition to be a journalist was short-lived, due in equal parts to immaturity and my inability to cope with the stress of the profession. I walked out of my journalism class, never to return. A heavy sadness enveloped me. I had truly wanted to write, to move people with my words and effect positive change. My parents had struggled to provide the money for my schooling, and my guilt weighed me down. Although I would still live at home, I began to cover all my own expenses.

I aimlessly took jobs wherever I could find them. Eventually, I found a job as a library clerk for a government office. Although I was hardly impressed with government bureaucracy, I stayed for two years.

Ironically, when I stopped trying so hard, my underlying goal of finding the right man—my soul mate—was realized. He was attending the college I had quit and a mutual friend fixed us up on a blind date. He was hairy—a physical attribute I deemed important when I was 18! Five years later, we wed, but not before I went back to college to become a paralegal. For the next eight years, I was an instrument in the wacky, non-stop world of real estate. Eating lunch and using the toilet facilities were luxuries! "Relief from the hectic pace was just a baby away," I recall thinking at the time.

Five years later our son was born. It was a logical decision between my husband and I that I would stay home. He was the greater bread-winner. We had old-fashioned values.

Being a mother was the hardest yet most exhilarating job I ever encountered. Often, I felt exhausted, frustrated, less than confident, dependant, depressed, lonely and not in control of my life. However, there were moments of such intense love I would cry. I could not believe that I could love my husband so much and then a baby could come into my life and my heart could swell to embrace that tiny being, as well.

We would spend our days together, doing mother-tot programs, reading, creating and trying to sleep. My son banged his head against his crib several hours a night from 14 months until two years of age. The diagnosis was a sleep disorder. I was so exhausted that some nights I would go to bed in my clothes, so I would be already dressed the next morning. I never had time for myself. My marriage was also being affected.

A nagging seed was beginning to grow in me, that I needed more in life to keep me buoyed, and I figured I was not the only mother who was slowly growing crazy. The sense of "brain rot" is a main impetus for many women to want to return to the workplace. Jan Brickman, whom I met over the Internet, was also a stay-at-home mother. She commented, "My brain was turning to mush...but my house was

spotless." (Not my house!) I had been naïve to think that only children could fulfill my inner soul.

At the time, my son was gaining two pounds each week. He was
like the 'Incredible Hulk' who busted out of his clothes. Every week I
was running to a budget store to buy cheap clothing for him that fell
apart when I washed it. After brainstorming with my husband, I
decided that what the world needed (and what I certainly needed)
were good quality 'grow clothes' for children: garments that would be
made with double sets of snaps up the leg, long roll-up cuffs, snaps in
the shoulders, wide sleeves...

After exploring the possibility with a marketing person who ran a
focus group for me, finding a designer, researching medical charts to
find out the average growth of children as infants and tots, and
acquiring a supplier of the material, my business was set to go. I
bought myself a sewing machine with the intention that I would learn
to make the clothing. What a ridiculous notion! My sewing experience was limited to a two-inch line to close up a pin cushion, and I
had failed miserably when I was in Home Economics (how many of
you are old enough to recall *that* class?).

The name of my company was Elinphantots Active Wear. I came
up with a logo: a hot pink elephant wearing a white diaper with an ice
cream cone in her trunk. I had 'iron-ons' of the logo created, which
we placed in the corner of each outfit, just like the famous IZOD alli-
gator. I had invitations made. The designer and I decided it would be
cute to have moms dressed in similar clothes. We used the primary
colors of red, green, blue and yellow in sweatshirt and jersey material.
My son was my model.

I sent out many invitations for an open house. The doors were not
busting down for people trying to get in to my open house. In fact,
only one person showed up. It would have been easy to pack it in.
Instead, I re-evaluated my marketing strategy. I bought a table at a
local craft and gift sale and the results were stupendous! Women ran

from their own tables to see my clothes. I had so many orders that I had to find a manufacturer quickly. A cousin connected me with a man from the fashion industry. Suddenly I felt like a small fish in a pond of sharks.

My career was to have been part-time. Yet, every morning I would drop my son off at my parents' home at 7:30 a.m. and return for him at 7:00 p.m. Since it was close to Christmas, many mothers insisted that they have the outfits ready to be under the tree. Bear in mind their children were only infants or up to four years of age. I was running around negotiating with too many people to have the final products ready in advance of the season, so that I could package them up. I had to pay the designer, the supplier, the 'snappers' (those putting on the snaps) and the manufacturer. Not only was I not making any money and running myself ragged, I was not spending time with my son. The guilt was creeping in. Within a year, I gave up the business.

I know in retrospect that I would have made money eventually. The product was worthy of my endeavor. I was proud of the fact that the supplier, who had not extended credit terms to his clients for years because of losses suffered previously, was so impressed with my idea, research and the fact that I was willing to put my own money into the business that he readily offered me the opportunity of partial credit. It felt good that I could do my own books efficiently, even though I earned a mere 30 percent in bookkeeping at high school!

Despite all the obstacles, I had managed to have those baby outfits under the tree for Christmas, thinking to myself, "Yes Virginia, there is a Santa Claus!" But more than any of that, for the first time in a long time, I felt empowered to have a life that was over and above just being a mom. I was respected out in the world where success was gauged on being an active taxpayer.

My husband and I were keen to have a second child, and when our son was three, we were delighted to learn that we were expecting again. Our daughter was born prematurely, at the same time we were moving to a new house and my son was to start nursery school. The combination of all three events put me over the edge. On the first day my son started nursery school, I did not cry—I was relieved. I believed I was an unfit mother.

Life returned to normal, but still I had 'ants in my pants.' I would say that I was a stay-at-home mom, but to me it seemed an oxymoron. I tried to organize friends in a support group, but nobody I knew was buying. I went outside my little world and phoned my local counselor to find out if a community support group could be set up. Timing was everything. They had just formed a steering committee looking into that very issue. They invited me to come to the first meeting and present my case. One thing led to another and I was connected with a group of women who were meeting in a church basement every week, informally, with their children. I convinced them that we needed a better place to meet, where stay-at-home parents or nannies could have a place to crash, learn or simply enjoy while their children were looked after.

We cut the ribbon for the Vaughan Child/Parent Resource Centre (now, 15 years later, there are two locations) a year later, after intensive research, planning, fundraising, purchasing and hiring. The sense of achievement was delicious. The centre was a place to relieve stress and make connections. I was part of something bigger than myself that was good for the community.

I continued to pursue avenues that would expand my world. I volunteered in my children's school. About six years into motherhood, a notice at my son's school caught my attention. They were looking for docents to take high school students through the 'Anne Frank in the World' exhibit. I was intrigued, but I did not know what a docent was. The secretary told me it was the European word for guide. I signed on and took the intensive study on Holocaust Education. It was not a subject ever discussed in any of my history classes at school. However, I had read *The Diary of Anne Frank* as a young teenager.

On day one of the exhibit, my head was buried in my script. It was the only way I could keep myself from shaking. "That was effective," I berated myself. "They must have been bored to tears." By day three, my confidence increased. I held my head high and ad libbed. Some of the teenage girls started to cry at the emotional content I was presenting. I had an epiphany. I was going to become a high school teacher. I would move people with my words, but in a different way. I was going to make the world a better place.

For the next three years (I waited until my daughter would be in school full-time), I immersed myself in Holocaust Education, the Parent/Child Resource Centre, arranged speakers at my children's schools for the parent nights, participated in other committees and volunteered with my high school English teacher (who was also involved in the Anne Frank exhibit) in her classroom. I was also a full-time wife and mother.

Finally, I was in university for my B.A. For five years, I loved learning, but I struggled to keep a balance. Visions of my college Journalism program reminded me of my shame of being a quitter. My husband was "the wind beneath my wings." Almost finished my plan (I still had to get into Education), my life veered again. I was diagnosed with breast cancer.

I had never lived my life in fear of getting cancer. When it happened, not only was it a shock, but the fear was all encompassing. My children were still needy. When do they ever stop being needy? The surgeon reassured me that my cancer was contained within a milk duct and that there was no evidence of metastasis. They would not even have to check my lymph nodes. I was told that I had a 97 percent chance that there would be no reoccurrence. I had great faith in my doctor's diagnosis, and so, with hope in my heart, I had a lumpectomy and radiation that summer.

In the fall, I graduated from university with honors, having made the Dean's List. I decided to take the year off before I applied to the

Faculty of Education. I sculpted my life to give me the experience necessary to gain access to Teachers College. I continued to volunteer in the high school, I ran a Pathfinder (Girl Guides, ages 12 to 15) group and tried to be the best mother and wife I could be.

I was elated when I was accepted into the Faculty of Education. However, my first practicum of being in the classroom full-time was abysmal. I hated it—the politics, government bills changing teaching methods, teacher strikes, work-to-rule, expectations of teaching a subject I had minimal knowledge of, learning lessons the night before I had to teach them (students get chastised for cramming, but for teachers it is an acceptable practice) and an unsupportive 'Mentor' teacher. What distressed me most were the students. They were rude, arrogant and unruly. If truth were told, as an old fogey (I was already almost 45!) I did not have the patience to be spending an inordinate amount of time disciplining students who had little apparent interest in learning. With the heaviest of hearts, I again abandoned my dream.

Depressed and with a persistent cold, within months I developed an oval-shaped rash under my arm. I alerted two doctors, as well as a radiation oncologist. I had read a plea from a woman in the newspaper who had an aggressive kind of cancer, which started as a rash under her arm. No doctor was alarmed. My mammogram was clear; therefore I was deemed cancer free. Three months after my rash had appeared, a lump appeared underneath it. It was the same side in which I had had cancer, two years prior. It was determined that cancer was now in my lymph nodes. I was high-risk.

Hope the second time was non-existent. I was angry that my lymph nodes were originally never checked. My daughter's Bat Mitzvah was three weeks after lymphadenectomy. Committed to proceed with the celebration, I danced at her party. Radical chemotherapy followed shortly thereafter. I recovered a year later, cancer free, grateful to be alive. And guess what? Cancer liberated my dream to write. I wrote an article about having humor and hope and filed it.

Serendipity! A chance reading of an editorial in an alternative health magazine published four months prior, spoke about the importance of following dreams. My dream was to get my article published.

Never being short on 'Chutzpah' (Yiddish for "utter nerve"), I called the editor and told her my dream. She cringed, I can imagine, probably thinking "you and everybody else." When I told her I was a second-time cancer survivor, she perked up and told me to send it to her. She agreed to publish it that summer. I thought I had won a lottery. (Proof positive that reading on the toilet can be good for your career!)

Buoyed by my good fortune, I proceeded to write another piece about being a cancer warrior. With assistance from a friend in politics, the article was published in my local newspaper with a large, colored picture of 'moi' and my story on a half page in the front of the community section. I had finally come home.

I knew I wanted to write; the question was for whom and how I would do it. The idea of freelancing was not something I was convinced about; I wanted something more stable. What is unbelievable to me now is that despite my years of achievement, I still lacked confidence in my abilities and worried that no one would want to hire me, an almost-50-year-old woman.

As a cancer warrior, I had to move on. My children were 20 and 17. My husband recognized my need to reinvent myself. Nevertheless, I feared entering the 'new workplace of high technology.' I had no idea where to turn to get help. By chance, I saw an ad in my local newspaper for a two-week course aptly called "Focus." The course was a career and employability workshop for women who had been out of the workplace for awhile and not collecting employment insurance. I thought 20 years qualified me! I enrolled in the two-week program and savored every moment of the learning experience. By the end of the session, my self-esteem soared.

The workshop offered self-assessment tests, which helped participants to determine our skills and passions. It provided insight into the myriad of occupations available, acknowledged our transferable skills—traits you have that you can take with you to the workplace, for example, organizational skills and communication skills (I was amazed I had any)—and provided oodles of emotional support to help us get through our fear of re-entering the workplace.

Compassion, humor and practical advice were the trademarks of all the facilitators, many of whom had overcome similar obstacles. I never knew how much help was available to facilitate re-employment until I took the Focus workshop.

Human Resources Development Canada (now known as Human Resources Skills Development Canada, HRSDC, and run locally by the Board of Education) funds the program. *See Resource section.* After intensive self-assessments, two things kept reoccurring: I loved to write and I had a passion for magazines.

I observed the women around me and saw the abject terror they felt about the prospect of going back into the workplace. We shared tears of fear. There was a story in there somewhere. I could just feel it bursting inside me. While taking Focus, I thought that since I loved writing and enjoyed reading magazines (they breed in my house), I would try my hand at being an editorial intern—a non-paying position to test if I wanted to work in the magazine industry. I researched magazines I thought would fit who I was. My immediate instinct was *Homemakers*. I was the consummate homemaker. I was so excited about the prospect. I did my homework thoroughly. I had all the criteria except one to get my foot in the door. The interview went splendidly until I asked the fateful question, "Does it matter if I am not going to use the internship for a diploma or degree?" The junior editor, lower down on the rungs of the hierarchy, thought not. However, the next day, she left a message saying that, indeed, it did matter and that she was sorry but I did not get the position.

Things happen in strange ways. *Homemakers* was merging with *Canadian Living* (both published by the same parent company), so that there would not be an overlap of material. My interviewer was losing her job at *Homemakers* but was moving over to a house and garden magazine. Upset that I did not get the internship but not defeated, it suddenly dawned on me that I had also applied to the same magazine for which my interviewer was now working. On a whim I called her, left a message saying that since she had already interviewed me and knew my capabilities, could she put in a good word for me to the other magazine editors? Whether it was coincidence or she actually did say something, I will never know because she never told me, the next day I was offered the internship at the house and garden magazine.

I followed up the Focus workshop with "Breakthrough," also a government project, run by the Academy of Learning. It centered on job preparation, including resume preparation, interviews, job-searching, networking, basic computer skills and staying motivated. In the fall of 2003, I became an editorial intern.

A few days before I started my internship, I panicked because I did not have QuarkXPress (a software program used for magazine publishing) computer experience. I never lied; the managing editor just did not ask, assuming I had that knowledge since I had some editorial background being editor of a newsletter at my son's school. Of course, that had been 13 years before and at that time we sent the newsletter out to be formatted and printed. I was almost a complete technophobe. My computer background was shaky at best.

A friend told me she knew an IT (information technology) person in the building. I was not able to meet her for a crash course, but she gave me valuable advice on who I could contact to retrieve any material I deleted by mistake. I held his name close to my heart!

Sure enough, on the third day, I was plunked in front of Quark and told to enter some articles written by others. I envisioned wiping out the whole magazine. I "saved" every time I typed a few words. I think it took me an hour to enter a two-paragraph blurb. When I discovered I deleted nothing, I rejoiced. I was even given a task to create an

Internet survey. The able woman, much younger than me who was the Web editor and had the patience of a saint, sat with me for an hour going over what I had to do. Being a visual and tangible learner, I carefully watched what she did and wrote down and numbered each step. By the end of the day, I had it down pat. It's not true that "you can't teach an old dog new tricks"!

While interning for a month, I became friendly with the editors of *Homemakers* magazine. My idea of writing a story for the magazine about women going back into the workplace, percolating inside my head for some time, was brought to the forefront. Many of the editors agreed that it was a good topic. When I was finally given to an assignment editor, she agreed it was important, but somebody else had scooped me. She would, however, allow me to do a 300-word sidebar for which I would be paid. I wrote the story, was paid, but never had the luck of seeing it in print.

Four things came out of my experience as an intern:

1.   I did not like the magazine industry, finding the constant stress of being on deadline overwhelming. It was also isolating.
2.   I did not want to work for someone else on a nine-to-five basis.
3.   I wanted to take a fact-checking course and learn the program that caused my greatest fear, QuarkXPress, at university.
4.   I wanted the story out into the world about women's fears of going back into the workplace.

I did take both the fact-checking and QuarkXPress course. Fact checking was exciting, Quark was not. I laughed when I got three out of 25 on my first test. Luckily, it held little weight in the scheme of things. I can honestly say that I know only slightly more about Quark than when I was first exposed to it. The challenge was in just doing it and getting the credit.

If I was not going to work for someone else, what was I going to do? Pitching the story to other magazines was not fruitful. A semi-autobiographical novel was practically writing itself in my mind, after my cancer experience. I had lost three friends to cancer and I needed a permanent place to honor them and to put into words my cancer journey. I proceeded to write *Ms. Humpty Dumpty*. (As of this printing, my novel has yet to find a publisher.)

The Learning Annex was offering a course on how to self-publish a non-fiction book by the famous American self-publisher Dan Poynter. Thinking it would help me with my novel, I attended. Before the course ended, I had a crystal-clear vision. I did not need to keep trying to convince magazine editors that I had a good story, and that women desperately needed something to help them get back into the world of work. I was going to write *the book*.

That night, *Women Reworked* was born in my mind. I thought, who better to write on the subject of getting back into the workplace than women who had gone through the struggle and had achieved success? I wanted their lessons to be shared with other women. Women need to know that they are not alone and that help is theirs for the taking— if they know where to look. There are many wonderful job-search books on the market. I did not want to compete with them. I wanted this book to be a resource guide, as well, with names, places and contact information. I never want another woman to be in the dark about going back into the workplace or changing careers.

It is *déjà vu*. At 51, a new episode in my 37-year quest for career happiness was about to begin. I am, at last, writing the words that I long to impart. My dream is now my reality.

Chapter 2

Fear

*No passion so effectually robs the mind of all its powers of acting
and reasoning as fear.*
    Edmund Burke, *On the Sublime and the Beautiful:* ll, ii

Fear can literally paralyze you from achieving success. For too often
and too long, that sense of self-doubt formed a black cloud over my
life. It was only when I found myself on the edge of life, with my two
experiences with cancer, that I overcame my fear and began to tackle
my dreams and seek help from other people. Do not wait until you
are in a life-threatening position to make positive changes in your life.
Living life to the fullest is a risk worth taking.

Whether you have spent time away from the workforce being a
mom, have traveled extensively with a spouse's job, have experienced
illness or even spent time in a penal institution, whatever the reasons
for having been away from employment for a lengthy period of time,
the next step for change is frantically frightful. I have also met women
who had high-powered corporate positions who decided that they
wanted to switch careers and saw such a move as "a scary prospect."

Even those tasked with hiring new staff for a company are afraid.
According to the famous job search book *What Color Is Your Parachute?*
by Richard N. Bolles, many employers are afraid of making bad hiring
choices. They just know how to hide their fear better than you do!
Anything that takes you out of your comfort zone will usually cause
great apprehension.

No matter what your past experience has been, if you have been out of the loop for several years, without a foot in the door, and want to get back in, your quest for employment becomes all the more difficult. Even women who have impressive backgrounds do not know how to get beyond their fears that they may lack necessary skills, have too many gaps in their employment history, be older than other women seeking positions, or lack the stamina to pursue a career.

D, 50, is one of these women. She has held three jobs in her life, one lasting for 24 years in administration. Undoubtedly, she had acquired many valuable skills along the way. She quit her last job over three years ago because of political issues she could no longer resolve in her mind. She enjoyed her decision for a year, but then started getting, in her own words, "brain rot." She discovered some government-funded, but locally run, employment programs to help her. With all the prep work, she still was petrified to look for a job.

I asked her the question: What are your fears and apprehensions about going back into the workplace?

"Mostly FEAR. Fear that I will not meet expectations (of either my employer or myself). That if I fail, it will do huge damage to my self-esteem. I am concerned about my age and that I will not measure up. In general, I am afraid of making mistakes or taking the wrong path."

D was so afraid that she became a professional student in re-employment courses for over two years. She finally realized the inevitable: there are only so many courses she could take to get her beyond her fears. The only way she was going to win the battle with fear, was to take the plunge. Her assessments in one of the programs helped her determine where her passions lay. She believed it was in the legal field. She received funding assistance, registered and completed a nine-month course, successfully, as a legal assistant. Her self-esteem was so low that it was a shock to her that she did so well.

She was hooked up with a job developer [see List of Terms] who helped her find a job in the legal industry. The developer asked her if she would be willing to look at other job possibilities. D told her only if the job was a good one. A job came up, but not in the legal field. D survived the first interview. She was asked back for two more, even though she was not convinced she had done well. D is now gainfully employed in a rewarding position that has room for growth. She has passed her trial period and is receiving benefits. Her organization, efficiency, excellent communication skills and dedication to her goal have served her well. In spite of that, she still lacks confidence that she is capable of doing the job. Why does she have such a self-deprecating attitude, even though her work ethic is high and everyone she has ever worked for was happy with her performance? D is not alone in her thoughts.

D,50, Markham, Ontario. This contribution, ©2005-2006, is used with permission.

Other women answered the question in a similar fashion:

"I am afraid that I am not capable enough to perform a job that interests me or that I can make a reasonable living from."

F, 26, Thornhill, Ontario. This contribution, ©2005-2006, is used with permission.

"I am terrified of this whole process....When I left the workforce, I never believed it would be hard to go back. After 10 years, I can't believe how difficult it seems. I worry about interviews—telling potential employers I have been away for 10 years; feeling that younger people will have an advantage; employers thinking that I won't be as committed because I am looking at shorter-term employment than others might be. In other words, this is not going to be a 25- or 30-year career for me."

Linda, 42, Winnipeg, Manitoba. This contribution,
©2005-2006, is used with permission.

"At times I am fearful of speaking in large groups, so I am willing to work my way up to larger and larger groups."

Tammy Karaim, 41, Motivational Speaker, Inner Lights P.O. Box Erin, Ontario N0B 1T0

1-519-833-2585. This contribution, ©2005-2006, is used with permission.

It is commonly said that people are more afraid of public speaking than dying. As comedian Jerry Seinfeld has joked, "They would rather be in the coffin than giving the eulogy!" If *you* are shy, read *The Networking Survival Guide* by Diane Darling.

The staff of the Focus Career and Employability Workshop (government funded) said that very often the women they see:

- fear failure and not being able to meet their goal;
- lack confidence and self-esteem and are worried what impression potential employers will have of them;
- worry they will not find work they want to do and enjoy;
- are afraid they won't get the remuneration rate they wish to receive;
- are concerned they will not be able to find work close to home (this is especially true for those who have school-age children);
- believe they will not find work that is purposeful;
- fear preparing for and conducting themselves in interviews;
- are afraid they will not find an employer willing to give them a chance to prove themselves and their skills.

The facilitator of the job search program Breakthrough (also government funded) said that many of the women she sees in the program are concerned that "I don't have any skills for the workforce" and "Nobody will employ me." She goes on to state that "the majority of women come into the group with a very negative approach to the job market, they lack self-esteem and confidence. They fear the change to their lives, some are angry they have to go back to work and they are very reactive to all the labor market trends."

Over and over again, I heard from women: "I feel like such a fraud. I am afraid that one day everyone will realize that I really can't do the job I have been doing. That it has just been a pretense." Somehow, as women, we have been socialized to believe that we are never good enough to make it. This belief may have been initiated by things said to us in the past and maybe even continued into the present or we have interpreted people's reactions as indicating displeasure.

While it seems like an oxymoron, many women also experience what amounts to a fear of success. Becoming successful when you may not have experienced it previously, is stepping outside your comfort zone. How will success affect your time and your relationships? Will you be able to manage your finances properly? These are all thoughts that could be lurking in your subconscious, potentially thwarting any opportunity for you to be successful. It is akin to the fear that somehow you are not worthy of success. It is important to confront the fear and rationalize its legitimacy. If you find you are truly paralyzed in moving ahead, it is vital to seek the help of a professional.

The good news is that women who have completed employment workshops recognize that "they are employable, have lots to offer an employer and feel far more confident and positive about their new challenge in life. They are more proactive as opposed to reactive," states Brenda Faktor, the facilitator of the Breakthrough Program. They are made aware and their feelings are validated by other women who face similar obstacles. Many women have gone on to set up their own networking and support groups amongst each other. They are motivated to carry out their action plan to meet their goals.

Stories abound of women who turned their panic into successful careers. To inspire you, I will give you some of those stories in the following pages. I will also tell you where to seek help in your quest for a career.

Chapter 3

Things to Consider Pre-Employment

Oh, how I wish I had a cheque-book of my own.

J.M. Barrie, *Peter Pan & Wendy*

It has been almost a century since Mr. Barrie penned these words from the mother of one of the "lost boys." That simple sentence is illustrative of women the world over yearning for financial independence to prove that they are worthy citizens. However, financial reasons are not the only ones that push women back into the workplace.

"My brain was turning to mush (but my house was spotless)," quipped Jan Brickman, a stay-at-home mother who responded to my question, "Why did you want to go back into the workplace?"

Perhaps the children are older and women need to find something to satisfy their own needs. For some women, it is to fill a void after a major life alteration, such as a divorce, death of a loved one, illness or retirement, or as a result of being fired or laid off. For others, it is to connect to the greater world. Paying taxes may not be our desired goal, but being a viable, contributing (thus paying) member of society is essential for many women's self-esteem.

I used to hate gym, especially the hurdles. No matter how low the hurdle was, it was too high for me. Short, stubby legs, left me sprawled on the ground. My classmates howled at the absurdity.

Hurdles are my metaphor. You have to take steps to get over them.
You can jump the hurdle and raise the bar,
then show the world YOU are a STAR.

It is time to follow lifelong dreams or discover your life purpose. Your journey begins now… What do you want to be now that you are grown up?

Many women have no idea what they want their ideal job to be. The first step towards re-entering the workforce is self-assessment. You need to know who you are, where you are in your life and where you would like to go, in order to define a career path. There are 10 key issues to consider:

1. What is your passion, what are your skills?
2. Do you want full-time or part-time work?
3. Would you consider self-employment?
4. Do your needs and values fit into a particular work environment?
5. What will be the financial cost of going back to work?
6. Will the time commitment be realistic?
7. Will there be a support system if you require it?
8. What does success mean to you?
9. Are you ready to set goals?
10. You will need a plan of action.

1. What is your passion, what are your skills?

Try this Exercise:

a) On a piece of paper, create four separate columns for things you: <u>Love to do</u> / <u>Like to do</u> / <u>Hate to do</u> / <u>Love to do but haven't</u> Jot down any items that come to your mind in each appropriate column. These can be from any area in your life—academics, your social world, activities with your children, hobbies, volunteering, relationships or relaxation, for example.

b) Once you've completed your list:
   • Ask yourself, "What would I like to eliminate?" Put a line or "x" through those things. For example, if you hate math, wanting to be an accountant may not be appropriate.

- Next, focus on the things you like to do and would be willing to explore. Highlight those items with a question mark (?).
- Highlight things you really love with an asterisk (*). Include things that others have told you that you are good at doing.

c) Re-examine your positive <u>Love to do</u> items (those you marked with an *). Start a new list with only those positive items, and add a column beside them titled <u>Skills</u> / <u>Attributes</u>. Beside each <u>Love to do</u> item, write what skills and attributes you used to accomplish each task. For example, if you volunteered at a seniors' home, you might list patience, organization, co-operation and commitment.

Next, ask yourself:
- How did I feel doing that activity?
- Did I eagerly anticipate returning to it?
- Did I grow from the experience?
- Did I get positive feedback from others?
- Could I see myself permanently doing that function?

For other possibilities, write the skills you think are necessary in a different ink color. Re-examine the list. Choose things you are passionate about. Eliminate those that did not live up to your expectations or that you would not like to pursue. Look at your abilities from all the things you have done and see how you can apply them to other areas of interest. These are called "transferable skills."

d) On a separate sheet of paper, you should list your <u>Values</u>. These are things like integrity, respect and equity, for example. Beside values, list your <u>Needs</u>. Do you need to be challenged, nurtured, physically active, for example?

e) Your last list is <u>Personal Characteristics</u>. Are you outgoing or reserved, creative, a team player…? What others say about you is also relevant to your profile.

Carefully examine your lists and combine them. A picture of who you are should begin to form, revealing employment that suits you. *See Resources under the section "Pre-employment—Free assessments and other career information" for on-line assessment quizzes.*

2. Do you want full-time or part-time work?

Does your career choice give you an option to choose either a full-time or part-time position? Do you require more money? Do you want to work full-time? Do you have time constraints due to other responsibilities?

3. Would you consider self-employment?

Only you and your family can determine this. There are many things to consider about self-employment [*see Chapter 21*]. Examine your skills (based on your self-assessment) and see if you have what it takes to own your own business.

4. Do your needs and values fit into a particular work environment?

Reassessing your values and needs from your lists above will help determine the kind of environment you want to work in. For example, if your need is to work in a small, nurturing environment, with flexible hours, it may not be in your interest to join a large corporation, where the hours are set.

However, job seeking also means being a **visionary** and having a **willingness to take risks**. Before you reject something unfamiliar, consider all the benefits and detriments. Are you willing to stretch the limits of your expectations for personal growth and skills development? Unless there are concrete reasons why you cannot do this, it would be beneficial to keep an open mind and review all possibilities. **Flexibility and adaptability** are among the top 10 skills that employers are seeking.

5. What will be the financial cost of going back to work?

Transportation:
- Bus fare
- Extra gas
- Wear and tear on the car (equals more car repairs)
- If you have only one car in the family and your spouse or someone else requires it, or if you do not own a car, you may need to purchase one if buses are not accessible for times and distance

Clothing:
- New or more complete wardrobe
- Dry-cleaning costs

Food:
- Lunches out or socializing after work

Office Pools:
- Putting in money for gifts, charities, and so on

Daycare for children, pet care or home care for seniors

Housecleaning

Haircuts, manicures

Upgrading your education

6. Will the time commitment be realistic?

Are you willing to commute long distances? What if the job involves travel, moving? Are you prepared to stay late for meetings, appointments? Would you bring work home, work on weekends? What about going back to school or upgrading skills? Will you be able to balance your personal needs and work?

7. Will there be a support system if you require it?

Who will be there to help you deal with things that are your responsibility now, including childcare, car pooling, cooking meals, housecleaning, pet care, senior care? When things get hectic, will you have the emotional support to keep you going? If you have a significant other, how will they feel about you switching gears? How will it affect your relationship? Statistically, women who do not have a support system will be less able to cope with the extra demands that arise when they return to the workplace.

8. What does success mean to you?

Assuming you worked out all of the above issues, and you landed a job of your dreams, how would you handle your success? Be careful what you wish for. You can be so caught up in the career you love that it can take over every aspect of your life. Balance is the key to survival.

Try to set a moral imperative for yourself, such as how many hours a day you are prepared to work, recognizing the need to be flexible. If making lots of money is a goal, put it into proper perspective. Many people who have lots of money are not happy people because they never have time to enjoy it or share it. A career should be something you love, not an obsession.

9. Are you ready to set goals? *See next chapter.*

10. You will need a plan of action. *See next chapter.*

There are many on-line career planning sites. Some provide complete career planning, while others only give limited services, such as self assessments. In addition to helping you find valuable information on how to get a job, they can also offer you:

- anonymity, if you are feeling uneasy about confronting others;
- a journaling resource—you can print out your answers to on-line questionnaires and save them as a reference for your changing needs;

- immediate suggestions to assist you in formulating a plan to get on track;
- savings in time and travel costs.

People Need People

Although you can plan your career without ever having to leave your house, it is not necessarily the most advantageous thing for you to do. Looking for a job is a person-to-person activity. Numerous places offer employment-search training, some geared specifically to the needs of women. By connecting with other women, you will:

- realize you are not alone;
- effectively network and build relationships;
- brainstorm ideas and solutions for job search issues;
- have a sense of purpose and opportunity to get out of the house;
- find other resources;
- boost your confidence;
- obtain constructive feedback;
- learn valuable people skills, including effective communication/listening, appropriate body language, dressing for success, and interview techniques.

Governments at all levels appear to be committed to successfully moving women into the workplace. There are many excellent programs and services available to assist you in your job search. Many government programs are free or at minimal cost to the participant. Finding the information is sometimes a daunting task, however. In this book, I have tried to ease your burden by providing you with the resources you will need to land your perfect career.

Chapter 4

Setting Goals and Creating an Action Plan

You have carefully considered all the pre-employment quandaries. You have an idea of who you are and what kinds of things would make you happy. Now, set some goals.

Setting goals and then creating an action plan is like drawing a map that will show you how to get where you want to go. It is a concrete way of checking to see if you are on the right track. Your inner motivation derives from knowing that you are taking positive steps and empowering yourself to take control of your life and the way you wish to live it.

Goals are not written in stone. Shape them to fit the lifestyle that you construct for yourself. If you are observant and allow new ideas to enter your realm, a completely new world of wonderful ideas can open up. On your search, you may discover a way of creating a career that you had never thought of before. For example, you may start out believing that you want to work for somebody else, based on your self-assessment, but your exploration has led you to find a niche that no one else has tapped into yet, and you may have the solution. With careful planning, dreams can become a reality.

Everyday, check over your goals, see what you have accomplished, what worked and what didn't work—and rework the next day's goals if necessary. Do not forget to celebrate all your daily achievements; consider having a relaxing bath, watching a favorite movie or listening to music that soothes your soul. Most importantly, talk with your friends and family; get feedback and keep putting one step in front of the other. You will reach your goal, but it requires diligence and the awareness that bumps in the road are inevitable. **The harsh reality of looking for a job is that you should be spending at least six hours a day exploring all avenues. It is hard work and can be frustrating. Surround yourself with positive people who can help you achieve your goals.**

The following text on goal setting is by Dr. Judy Goss, and is modified from the article "Sports Psychology Consultant New Year's Resolutions" in the March/April 2004 edition of *Active Woman Canada.*

• • •

Goals have to be specific and realistic. Use positive, specific words to describe what you want to do or be. **Goals need to be written down and posted where you can see them. Let others know of your commitments**. For example, your ultimate goal should be, "I will be gainfully employed in the career of my choice [if you know the specific career, name it] within six months and not "I would like a job right away."

Set mini-goals, for example:

"During this week, I am going to job search."

"By the end of this week [or within a feasible time], I will find out where I can get help."

"I will prepare to follow through with the advice that is being offered to me."

Make a copy of your goals and give it to someone you trust. In six months (or whatever time you determined your main goal would be accomplished), have that person mail your goals back to you. Did you accomplish your goals? Congratulate yourself if you did, and celebrate. If you did not, ask yourself why, and try to rectify it.

Goals are ineffective unless you have an action plan **in writing**. It needs to be specific and timely.

- Use a manual daily planner or a computer planner.
- Only put in the amount of things you can do that are realistic for your life.
- Plan what you will do.

- Refer to it the day before so you will know what you will be doing the next day.
- Try to stick to this schedule.
- Plan appointments so that you have time to get to them, not too many in one day.
- Cross out things as you do them.

Getting a job requires the assistance of others. Use all sources available to you. Remember to exercise, eat and get enough sleep.

• • •

Sample Action Plan

Monday:

Make a list of all the people I know, to ask for their help in getting a job. I will contact as many of those people as possible.

Tuesday:

Go to the library, speak to the librarian for books and resources about getting a job. Check the Internet.

Wednesday:

Contact as many of the sources provided to me as possible.

Thursday:

Register for government programs I was told about, that I believe would be helpful.

Friday:

Get supplies I need for the registered programs. Continue speaking to people about finding a job.

If you know the career you want, your action plan may look something like this:

Monday:

Check advertisements in the papers for jobs in my area of interest to see what requirements are necessary for the job. Determine if I have those skills, and if not, find out what I need to do to attain them.

Tuesday:

Research companies on the Internet, at the library, and so on, that employ people in a similar career.

Wednesday:

Call as many companies as possible to make a contact, so I can arrange information interviews. [These are interviews that you arrange with people in the industry that you wish to explore. They do not have to be people you know.]

Check out:

- companies found on the Internet
- other people
- libraries
- the Yellow Pages

Take the following steps:

1. Call the company and talk with the receptionist.
2. Tell them your name and what your purpose is.
3. Ask them to whom they recommend you speak.
4. Try to connect with that individual and arrange a time to meet.

Thursday:

Check newspapers and magazines to spot trends in that industry.

Friday:

Meet four contact people for information-gathering interviews within easy traveling distance of one another.

These interviews should **never** go over fifteen minutes and should be at their convenience. Keep the questions general, for example:

- how they got into the business;
- what they like about it;

- what they do not like about it;
- what is required to get into the business;
- do they consider that there is a future in this business.

Ask for referrals to talk to others, and don't be afraid to take notes. Make sure you tell the person you want to interview that you will only require fifteen minutes of their time because you are exploring the industry and that they were referred to you as the perfect person to talk to. Most people are flattered that they were chosen by you as an authority and do not mind giving some time. Ask for their business card. Send out thank-you e-mails and cards to anyone who gave you an informational interview.

When you interview people in a prospective industry of your choice, bear in mind a few things. They are only giving you their personal opinion. If the individual likes or dislikes their job, that will be reflected in what they say about it. They could be having a good or bad day or be busy. Their knowledge may be limited to their specific job. Their comments should be taken together with the opinions of others, your own research and how you feel about the career. It is like a marriage: You do not know somebody until you live with them. You cannot know with certainty that the career is for you unless you experience it.

Evaluate your progress regularly periodically and have backup plans. You are closer than you think!

Chapter 5

Networking, Networking, Networking

Please, please, please emphasize the importance of networking before you take leave, while you are on leave and after you go back. Word-of-mouth is key in getting a job, being moved laterally and being promoted. It is essential to those who choose to be self-employed.

Lillian D. Bjorseth, author, speaker, trainer
President of Duoforce Enterprises, Inc.

Business Networking Business Development, Communication Skills
www.duoforce.com e-mail lillian@duoforce.com Lisle IL
This contribution, ©2005-2006, is used with permission.

Eighty percent of the job market is hidden. That means that most job opportunities are not advertised, and the ones that are, get thousands of applicants. How is an employer to choose *your* resume over the mountain of others? It is a far better suggestion and more efficient to begin networking with people you know, those who they know, and individuals you do not yet know, to find employment. It is imperative for job-search success to learn the tools of the networking trade, no matter how uncomfortable you might feel.

Networking is not about just walking into a room, going up to somebody, handing them your business card and saying, "Hi. I am looking for a job. Can you help me?"

Learn about the person you are talking with. Simply have a conversation. If things click between you, it will usually happen instantaneously. Cards should be exchanged only if the person asks for it. People usually end up with piles of cards and they cannot remember who the person is. Most cards are either dumped in the garbage, or the recipient can't locate it when they need it. If you do a card exchange, mark on the card where you met that person, the date and anything about that person that you should remember. Follow up and send thank-you e-mails or cards to anyone who has been helpful to you.

A colleague of mine, Donna Messer, the "queen of networking," who is president of ConnectUs Communications Canada and author of the best-seller *Effective Networking Strategies,* has this message for newcomers to networking: "People respond to others they like or who are like them." Build a relationship of trust and respect. Find your common ground and you can build on that relationship. How can you be mutually beneficial for each other? You may not be able to help that person immediately, but perhaps you will have an opportunity to do so at some other time down the road.

Some of the stories in this book were passed along to me because I networked with the right people. Advice that I have received while writing this book came to me frequently because I knew who had good information and I sought their guidance. However, I was also prepared to listen and learn from those who advised me.

The following is my advice for successful networking:

- Choose your networking event carefully. Not all sessions are going to be good for you.
- Go in with a positive attitude.
- Take bold steps to approach someone you do not know.
- Rather than saying, "What do you do?" ask them what their passion is. That is sure to spark conversation.
- Listen to what they say.
- Have a 20- to 30-second blurb ready that describes who you are

and what it is you are looking for. This has to be specific. "I need a job" implies that you will take anything regardless of whether it is what you want.

- Support the people you network with by using their products or services.

- Read about all kinds of things daily. Not just for knowledge or entertainment but to see if there is something in what you read that could possibly be a resource for yourself or for someone else. Share something valuable with others.

- If you say that you will give someone a resource, follow up immediately when you get home or tell them when you can get the information to them. They will be appreciative and some-times even surprised that you actually did what you said you would do. If you cannot help, do not offer to do so. Honor is becoming a lost art. It is an amazing feeling knowing that you have given someone important information that helps them in some way.

- Do not pretend to be something you are not.

- Use a business-card holder that can hold several cards but is small enough to tote around. When you get home, put the cards into a binder with plastic sheets. Each sheet holds 20 cards. You can organize cards into categories, making them even more acces-sible. Just flip through the pages to find a card that you need.

- Wear a card necklace where you can store your own cards and they are readily available to hand out. To find one of these, check corporate novelty businesses, for example, those that put logos on pens.

- Sometimes it is not possible to wait to build up a relationship. You may need to ask someone for certain information that you require immediately. Having said that, it does not mean, nor should it mean, that what you are asking cannot be mutually beneficial.

"But, I'm shy," you say. Diane Darling, in her book *The Networking Survival Guide,* offers helpful advice. She says that shyness is a learned response from things that have happened to us in our past. With some effort, the negative feelings you harbor can be purged. Sometimes you have to get outside help to do this. There are things that you can do for yourself, including the following:

- Try to understand what you fear.
- Replace negative thoughts with positive ones.
- Keep up your world knowledge in as many subjects as possible by reading newspapers, magazines and books, listening to radio and watching television (it is easier to talk to someone if you know about many things).
- Make a point, where possible, of stepping out of your comfort zone, for example, by speaking to a stranger in a store about a particular product—ask what they know about it, and if they use it. Then thank them for their help.
- Prepare three questions in advance of an event that you can ask someone (they do not have to be business related).
- Genuinely be interested in what others have to say.

A great way to become an effective speaker and comfortable with other people is to join your local Toastmasters Association. I have only ever heard wonderful things about it. http://www.toastmasters.org/ e-mail toastmasters@xmr3.com

In his famous job-search book *What Color Is Your Parachute?,* Richard Bolles states that we all have a passionate subject that makes us comfortable. He suggests finding someone you do not know who has the same interest. For example, if you are interested in bird-watching, look in your business section of your phone directory for something in that category or phone a conservation area and ask someone if you can arrange to meet with them to discuss your mutual interest. He emphasizes that you should tell them that you will not take up more than 10 minutes (and stick to it!) of their time and be honest about why you want to talk to them—that you are practicing your speaking skills or that you want information. Bolles says that it is okay to bring people with you if you are feeling very uncomfortable and let them take the lead of the conversation, with you actively listening and learning.

If you go alone and are unsure of what to say, he suggests asking how they got involved in birdwatching. What do they like about it? Is there anything they dislike about it? After listening carefully, you can describe your interest. Ask for references of other people you can talk to and if you can say that they have referred you. Would they mind calling the person in advance to ask if it is all right if you go and speak to that person? Thank the person for their time. Keep practicing this skill until you feel comfortable talking with others. The key in any interview, Bolles emphasizes, is to be enthusiastic.

There are hundreds of networking groups from which to choose. All you need do for an Internet search is type in networking organizations and where you live to see what comes up. If you are interested in a particular field, just look up that field on the Internet to see what is available to join. Groups can range from casual to formal, where you meet on a specific date of the month, and sometimes with a dinner and speaker. There is time allotted before and after the speaker to get to know one another. There are even networking cruises that are being organized!

Virtually every profession has an association where networking plays a vital role in successful careers. Some of these networking groups can be costly with initiation fees and monthly expenses if there is food or a speaker involved. Some government-sponsored employment programs or community-oriented organizations have networking groups that may not cost any fee, but you many need to be referred from another social service.

Select your networking groups carefully to fit your specific needs. You have to feel comfortable with the people who are in the group. It is unrealistic to expect to maintain hundreds of relationships. The most important thing to remember is that networking can happen anywhere you are. Be ready and open to let people into your life, where you can build a working relationship. If you learn to ask for what you need and learn to give in return, your life will be rich in successes.

Chapter 6

Knowledge Is Power

By reading Chapters 2 through 5 of this book, hopefully you will have:

- discovered who you are;
- determined your needs and what makes you passionate;
- set your goals;
- prepared an action plan;
- researched where you might find help; and
- learned the importance of networking.

Congratulations on taking the necessary steps to get you closer to finding your dream career!

You are confident because you have taken the time to put all the tools in place. The assistance provided has given you a clear sense of purpose. You are ready to hold your head high and show the world that you have something vital to offer. It is now time, as Nike says, to "Just Do It"— the actual job search.

Before you plunge into a particular field, you should learn as much as you can about it. There are numerous ways to do this.

Read about the industry in **books, magazines and newspapers.** There are many things you will discover when you are reading business material. You will take note of new businesses and those that are expanding; you will learn why they are successful, the values by which they operate and the problems that are particular to that industry. You will discern industry trends and you may discover a field you previously haven't known about or haven't considered for yourself. You will glean contact information, and you will have earned a sense of confidence in any interview setting.

The cost to you for all of the above benefits? Pretty close to zero, unless you wish to purchase the material or make photocopies. Libraries contain many valuable resources and should be utilized extensively. You can also browse bookstore shelves to take note of popular titles.

To keep organized, make your notes in a notebook or on a laptop computer. Record the date, where you saw the material, the name of the resource, anyone you spoke with, and so on. Little pieces of paper or Post-it® Notes get lost in the shuffle.

Brochures/Pamphlets are also excellent sources of information, most notably contact information, and will often provide you with key points about a company. Bear in mind, however, they are written with a specific spin to them. They are advertisements in a different form.

The information contained in brochures and pamphlets is concise, and you may find you will use the contact information from the printed piece to expand your research into the company and the industry in general. Keep this type of material organized in a binder or folder that is labeled and then file alphabetically in a box or filing cabinet.

If you enjoy using the **Internet**, it is like having a library at your fingertips. A great free service is Google™ News Alerts.

1.   Go to the Google™ Web site
2.   Click on the word News, on top
3.   Click on News Alerts icon on the left side of the screen
4.   Type in what you want information on; for example, key in a company name or a career (if you want information from another country, specify your word and the country), whether

you want Web information, news or both, how often you want to be notified and your e-mail address. Every time your words are mentioned in the source you choose, you will be alerted about the information.

5.   Click Create Alert. I get daily articles from newspapers and other publications around the world about women reentering the workplace.

To use the Internet generally, type in specific company names, industries, fields, career profiles and Google™ people's names. There are often links you can pursue, as well. This is an especially useful tool to use when seeking specific information about a company that will be giving you an interview. It is important to show that you have knowledge of the company. Information you can often access includes:

- company mandates;
- owners, directors;
- the culture of the organization;
- information about products or services;
- benefits and perks;
- financial stability (if it is a public firm);
- branch locations;
- the company's future plans.
- career opportunities

• • •

A word of caution: Not all information on the Web is accurate or even authentic. The following tips to help determine Web legitimacy have been modified from the book by Janet E. Alexander and Marsha Ann Tate, *Web Wisdom: How to Evaluate and Create Information Quality on the Web.* It is just a guide. There are legitimate Web sites that do not feature all of the things mentioned here.

Authority of Site

- Is there ownership for the site—company, organization or person (a logo)?
- What are their qualifications to write the material on the site?

- Is contact information included?
- Is there a copyright holder?
- Does the site have recommendations, ratings or testimonials from external sources?

Accuracy

- Is the site free from errors—grammatical, spelling or typographical?
- Can facts be verified from an original source?
- Are any graphs, charts or tables easy to read?

Objectivity

- Is there a clarity in point of view?

If there is advertising:

- Is the relationship between advertiser and owner of the site made apparent?
- Is there a clear difference between information and advertising on the page?
- Does the site have an explanation of policy relating to advertising and sponsorship?

Pages with non-profit/corporate sponsor:

- Are the names of non-profit or corporate sponsors made clear?
- Does the site have links to non-profit or corporate sponsors?
- Is the nature of the sponsorship disclosed (for example, non-restrictive, educational)

Currency

- Is the date of current material shown?
- Is there a date that the information was first placed on the server?
- Are dates (or times, if appropriate) of revisions indicated?

Coverage and Intended Audience

- Is it clear what materials are included on the site?
- If the page is under construction, is there an expected date of completion?
- If there is more than one intended audience for the material, is the material clear for each audience type?

Interaction and Transaction Features

- Is there a Secure Financial Policy, if transactions are possible?
- Is information being asked of user? If so, is use of information explained? There should be a clearly stated confidentiality policy.
- Is there a mechanism for feedback on the site?
- Are restrictions about downloading and other uses clearly stated?

• • •

Industry newsletters, whether print or on-line, and magazines, free or subscription-based, are excellent sources of information that can assist you in learning more about an industry that interests you, including current trends, and in searching for employment opportunities. They can also provide you with the opportunity to post and circulate your own employment needs or to submit articles for publication.

Industry-specific chat lines and blogs are trendy sources of information these days. However, it is wise to keep in mind that these may be informal and the person at the other end is expressing a *personal* point of view. Negative comments made about employers or potential employers can get you fired—or not hired.

To find out what industries are expanding—meaning hiring—what new industries or occupations will arise in the near future, salaries, employment practices, education requirements for careers. You need to research **trends in the industry**. This is also known as Labor Market Information (LMI). Reading business sections of newspapers, business magazines, asking a librarian to recommend books/Internet sites or typing into the computer "labor market trends" and your area will provide you with ample information to help you determine if the career you are considering is worthwhile. It will also give you information on other careers to ponder.

Statistics can be valuable tools if used correctly. If you are interested in 'crunched' numbers related to an industry, go to [**Statistics Canada** http://www.statcan.ca/start.html or **FedStats** for U.S. http://www.fed-stats.gov/]

To get an understanding of an industry you have to **talk to the people who work in it**. [*See Chapter 4 for "informational interviews."*] You can also do this informally at networking meetings or any social gathering.

Remember, it may just be one person's opinion, and whether they love or hate their industry could make a difference in what they say. Listen to many people and then come to your own conclusions.

Lectures and workshops are often advertised in newspapers and magazines, on university or college bulletin boards, or through community centers. Often there is a fee to attend, so if money is an issue, you will want to choose only the ones you believe will be the most beneficial. To get information without attending, check to see if there is a contact person, connect with them and tell them that you are not able to attend but you are interested in the subject. Ask them if they have any material they can provide you. If there is a fee involved, be honest about your financial situation and you may get a sympathetic ear. You have now made a new contact as well!

Job fairs are a successful and more recent concept wherein many employers gather in one place in order for recent graduates and other job seekers to access information about their companies and particular jobs. The job fair setting can give you the opportunity to view many different companies all at one time. Check newspapers and trade magazines for notices of upcoming job fairs.

Enhancing your formal education through an educational institution is both costly and time-consuming, so do as much research ahead of time to feel confident that it is your chosen career path. Check trends in that industry to determine your prospects of securing a job upon completion of your diploma or degree. If you can access them, co-op programs are often ideal, allowing you to gain practical experience in the workplace as well as theory.

Virtually every industry has **associations/organizations** specific to the field. Membership in these groups can sometimes be costly; however, often a prospective member can attend a small number of meetings as a "guest" either for free or for a small fee.

Internships are often available for recent graduates from a particular program. You might get paid for these training positions and you will have to commit a certain amount of time. Research the industry for specific information on these opportunities.

Apprenticeships are connected most often with technical jobs. You are trained by the employer or an association in order to learn a particular skill. These are usually paid positions and require passing an examination to qualify for certification. Research the industry for specific information on these opportunities.

Volunteering *[See Chapters 18 and 19, as well as Resources section of this book]* is an excellent way to learn or reinforce skills, try different jobs, make contacts and perhaps secure paid employment in future. It is usually connected with the non-profit sector, but **be bold** and ask if a prospective employer would consider you volunteering with them for a brief period of time, up to three months, for example. If you don't ask, you will never know!

Another thing you can do is volunteer in a non-profit organization related to an industry you wish to be employed in. For example, you want to work for a pharmaceutical company that makes cancer drugs. Consider volunteering for a cancer organization that may need help in typing research reports or where you have access to information that can help you expand your knowledge of the industry.

Sitting on a board, council, committee or advisory group, either in a non-profit or for-profit organization, can make good sense as you seek to reenter the workplace. Each organization will have specific qualifying criteria.

Why Work So Hard to Find a Job?

Perhaps you have been out of work for a lengthy period of time. You may be feeling that you are not making a valuable contribution to the world. You may feel depressed, lethargic or financially pinched. Instead, try thinking of this period in your life as a gift of time. It has taken you this long to get to the point you are at, so why not take a little longer to explore the possibilities of keeping your dream career in sharp focus. **You are a worthy investment.** Even if you require a survival job (for immediate financial reasons), you should try to secure a job you enjoy and one with room for emotional and career growth.

Nothing is ever certain, but the more you know about what it is you want in life, the more successful you will be. If you move with too much haste and not enough knowledge, you may find yourself getting into something you recognize all too quickly as not being right for you.

Chapter 7

Advice From the Other Side: The Employer
Anne Winter Mazurier's Story

Playing politics in a dog-eat-dog world of employment may be the name of the game today, but Anne Winter Mazurier achieved her success the good old-fashioned way—with hard work, focus and big-picture vision. Her story can serve as a guide to career fulfillment.

Originally from England, Anne had a college degree in commerce with languages (affiliated to London University, but less than a B.A.). Wanting to "perfect" her French, she moved to Paris, found love and married.

Anne left a career with a "well-paid, administrative and Human Resource (HR) management position working in Paris, France," having worked herself up from a secretarial position. She divorced and subsequently remarried. The newlyweds moved to London. Her husband preferred a domestic wife. She accepted this since they wanted a family and she had two children from her previous marriage.

"I came to Canada as a trailing spouse (pregnant and with a 14-month-old toddler)," she recalls, having been out of the workplace for three years. The year was 1978. Her husband had accepted a position and both were eagerly anticipating their Canadian adventure.

Anne did all the usual stay-at-home things—mothering, volunteering, home decorating… When all her children were older and in school, she suddenly felt those things "were insufficient to fulfill me." Another warning bell was going off simultaneously. Her husband was experiencing "job-related and financial difficulties." He turned to the bottle. "Having been out of the workplace for eight years, I insisted on going back to work to pay off bills, retain my independence and ensure a good life for my children."

Her dual languages were an asset, but her previous work had been too far in the past to land her a job in Human Resources. Starting from the bottom at age 46, she took a "low-paying survival job to pay the bills and gain Canadian experience." From there she progressed to a better paying secretarial job. She did not enjoy secretarial work, remembering how happy she felt working in Human Resources. Nevertheless, she realized that her move to secretarial was a means to an end. Her work ethic landed her an Executive Assistant position in a larger corporation, which had benefits. One perk, in particular, caught Anne's' eye: a tuition reimbursement program.

"I always had a complex about not having a university degree, even though I had had a successful, high-profile career in Paris." Given a chance to remedy her insecurity, at 49 she continued to work full-time while attending McGill University at night in the HR Management program. Making the honor list, she finished the four-year program in a record two years. Her graduation two years later opened up new opportunities at the company where she was employed, albeit on the lowest rung of the HR ladder. Once again, Anne proved her ability to grow and adapt. She headed projects with more responsibility, soon becoming a manager. Her boss was her morale booster. "I owe a great deal to my boss at the time (now deceased) who encouraged me all the way."

However, good things sometimes come to an end. Her company had a massive layoff and Anne was one of its casualties. Now fully confident of her abilities, she sought and became a manager and eventually a Director of HR. It was at that point in time that Anne's efficiency, communication, organizational skills and ability to "rally the troops" with motivation, was starting to be noticed by others in the industry.

A headhunting firm contracted by a company found Anne, and
the company whisked her away where for almost five years she
served as Director of Human Resources and Executive Team
Committee Director. Anne was looking to her retirement from that
company in two to three years, but financial misfortunes meant
immediate layoff. Anne has decided to accept her traditional age
(65) retirement.

Her years of experience as a respected, diligent Human Resources
Director has given Anne a bird's-eye view of the human component in
the corporate setting. "Over the course of my work in Paris, I discovered that contented employees made the work environment agreeable
and most certainly contributed to the bottom line. I really enjoyed the
people aspects of managing."

Anne attributes her success to the following:
- an ability to gain the trust and confidence of the employees;
- insistence on open communication;
- expectations of fairness and consistency;
- a practice of involving people in decisions, including surveying
  employees and acting on their comments wherever possible

Sage advice from Anne: "Listening always leads to success."

Anne was 60 when she got her last position—almost an unimagin-
able scenario in the corporate world where people are expected to
retire at that age, and there is pressure to "hire someone younger to
middle-aged." Her last employer, however, was looking for someone
more experienced to guide the company and was willing to concede to
her knowledge. Anne has much wisdom to impart.

Anne aced her interview with her last employer (even though she
was headhunted, she still had to go through four interviews), and she
agreed to share six key tips for interview preparation:
1. Research the company, the product.

2. Prepare questions to focus the hiring manager on what he actually expects (and wants done by the successful candidate).

3. Dress for success, for example, a business suit, fashionable shoes and matching accessories.

4. Within the interview discussion, weave in details of your education upgrading, especially if you did well or finished sooner in a particular program.

5. Talk about the experience you have in the field.

6. Impart your passion for the field and "leave the impression of a healthy, energetic competent candidate with relevant experience who would be a great fit for the job."

Using these tips, you will find that after the interview, you will have a better idea of what challenges the position would hold. Be prepared to show how these would be dealt with should you get the job. If you have met your potential boss, consider how comfortable you would feel working with the company. Always thank her for her time, mentioning that you enjoyed the conversation and reconfirming your interest in the position.

Multiple interviews are increasingly common in the selection and hiring process. The following is an example of the process:

Interview 1—Introduction and information exchange;

Interview 2—Anticipating questions and deciding which anecdotes or examples to use to illustrate how you might solve a problem;

Interview 3—Confirming that you are the right person;

Interview 4—Final—Meeting the team that you will be working with.

Anne leaves us with these parting words of wisdom:

• Decide what your interests are.

• Find out what it takes to be qualified in that field.

• Take the steps to acquire the necessary qualifications (hard work and sacrifice to be sure). It helps to keep telling yourself that it is an investment that will pay off handsomely to secure a better job doing something you like, that it will form character (self-discipline), raise self-esteem and earn the admiration of family and friends.

- Be prepared to take a lower paying job, with perhaps less responsibility, to develop your skills.

- Your resume should be clear and well-written, no longer than two pages. All gaps in time should be accounted for, including time spent raising your family, if appropriate. Make note of any volunteer work and upgrading of your education during that time.

- Your covering letter should highlight the criteria especially requested in the ad, if applicable.

- Display a positive, confident and pleasant outlook at the interview. It must come naturally for you to feel comfortable talking about your resume. Practice, practice, practice.

- Never, ever give the impression that you do not believe you will get the job because of being out of the workforce for too long, or that you may be too old. This can be a self-fulfilling prophecy. Concentrate on persuading the interviewer that you are interested, capable and motivated, and that you consider the absence an enhancing and positive experience rather than a deterrent to becoming employed!"

Anne concludes: "Women should concentrate on their strengths not weaknesses. Remember that bringing up a family or doing volunteer work can demonstrate organizational skills very successfully. It also reveals experience in decision making, problem solving, meeting deadlines, dealing with the unexpected, managing a budget, and more— the same kind of things experienced in a previously paid job."

Anne Winter Mazurier, 65, Brockville, Ontario.

This contribution, ©2005-2006, is used with permission.

Interview Savvy

Your next step—the job interview—will probably cause you the most worry. If you feel intimidated at the prospect of sitting across from a potential employer trying to favorably impress them into hiring you, you are not alone.

The key to successful interviewing is preparation. The more you know walking into that all-important meeting, the more you will feel in control, calm and confident.

Practice, practice, practice

Prepare for the interview:

Research the prospective company thoroughly.

- Check out their Web site.
- Read their financial reports, if a public company.
- Read articles about the company.

Memorize your resume, so you do not seem surprised when they ask you a question about it.

Carefully prepare questions for the interviewer.

- For example, "I noticed from my research that you are expanding into the Asian economy. How do you plan to meld the cultural differences to ensure future success?"
- Or "How do you gage a successful person in this position?"

Prepare answers by anticipating questions they may ask you. Try to read between the lines of questions. You have to provide solutions for them.

- For example, from the interviewer: "Tell me about a difficult situation in your last job that you diffused?" The interviewer wants to know if you are able to solve problems with peers in an efficient, cost-effective manner.
- Or "Tell me about yourself."

They are really asking for a few examples of your personality traits and accomplishments that could benefit their company.

Do mock interviews several times with colleagues and other business people. Try to get these videotaped, if possible, and study these interview tapes to assess your body language and verbal responses.

Have all the supplies you need for the interview ready, for example suitable clothing, a pen and paper.

Know where you are going and how long it will take you to get there.

Know your legal rights regarding questions that you do not have to answer. These include asking your age, marital status, religion or sexual preference.

Your palms are dripping wet, your stomach feels like a construction site, yet as nervous as you may be, the interviewer is even more worried. According to Richard Bolles, author of *What Color Is Your Parachute?* many experts make bad choices when they hire. They just know how to hide their fear better than you do.

The following are some tips to help you reduce your anxiety:

- Breathe deeply and often;
- Dress confidently;
- Give yourself time to get to the interview. However, do not arrive at the actual site any earlier than 10 minutes ahead of your appointment;
- Have a relaxing non-alcoholic beverage away from the site, if you are too early. Brush your teeth or use a breath mint after;
- Think of the interview as an opportunity to gather information. You are also interviewing the interviewer to see if their company fits your values.

Seizing the Moment

Upon meeting the interviewer:

- Make eye contact long enough to notice the color of her eyes, while giving a firm handshake. **SMILE.**
- Observe something that could help you could break the ice. For example, if she displays many awards, say, "I see you have been awarded several times. What are they for?"
- Let the interviewer lead about the job position.

Remember, you are going to provide them with solutions. Give concrete examples of how your skills can benefit them. Why do you stand out from the crowd? For example, "In my previous job, I initiated a program that was cost-effective and timesaving, resulting in increased revenue for the company."

- Listen carefully.
- Respond skillfully from your memorized answers even to uncomfortable questions such as "Tell me a weakness that you have?" Turn this question into a positive. For example, "Sometimes I am impulsive, but I am learning to take the time to think before I react." **Taking a pause to think is better than blurting out something you will regret.**
- Ask questions in between about the company and particular job, but ones that you have not been able to find answers for in your research. For example, "What do you value most in an employee for this position?"
- The interviewer should be the only one bringing up salary and benefits.
- Ask directly, at the end of the interview, what the hiring process is and if they have any concerns about hiring you. You may be able to rectify their issues.

- **Thank them with a handshake and smile,** get their card and tell them you will follow up by a certain date.

Congratulations! You have successfully completed an interview. Send a thank you note within the same day by e-mail or hand written.

Advice From Top Employers

I am "relentless," according to an employee of one of Canada's Top 100 Employers, as listed in an annual publication and rated by the employees. I had contacted each one of these employers last year to see if they would give me some advice that I could pass on to my readers. Almost half responded to my six questions. One employee of a public relations firm was getting upset because I was following up on my original request. In an e-mail not meant for my eyes but for the manager of client support services, the woman asked her colleague "Should I e-mail this woman back and tell her we are just too busy at the moment to answer these questions? She is relentless." It gave me a great chuckle that a public relations company may have been ranked as one of the top 100, but the employees certainly were not.

Their answers to me were just as curt. I am glad that I am relentless; it is the only way to get things done. There is badgering and then there are gentle reminders. I chose to take the 'high road,' politely re-asking my questions and suggesting that if they did not have time to answer to just please let me know so that I would not waste their time. They chose to take the 'low road.' I am telling you this story because it is an illustration of how not to treat a prospective client or anyone else for that matter.

The employers that did answer my questions gave some pertinent advice:

- They all said that unless it was a basic entry-level job, the woman would have to have the necessary skills and qualifications for the job. That means that if you have your eye on a specific career, make sure that you have kept your skills up-to-date or are prepared to upgrade if necessary prior to the job interview. Keep current on labor trends.

- Women should not try to hide the gaps in their resume. They have to be honest about why they have been away from the workplace. When you are talking about this in an interview, emphasize all the skills you were using while away. For example, a mother would have organizational, time-management and multi-tasking skills. Employers are expecting these all-important soft skills from their employees. Volunteering is an important way to stay in the loop.

- Using temporary employment agencies is a good way to get your foot in the door of the company. You still have to have the necessary skills for the particular job, but you could try the position out to see if it is a fit for you. If you do well, it could turn into a permanent arrangement.

- If you know what career you want and have the skill set to do so, **Placement Agencies** are a great way to get your foot in the door of a company and to test the position to see if you enjoy it. The positions can be temporary, permanent or contract (based on a particular period of time or a specific project).

- Make sure you do your research on the company. Show that you are interested in that company.

- The top 10 soft-skill requirements expected:
  1. team player
  2. multi-tasker
  3. problem solver
  4. excellent written or oral communications
  5. flexible
  6. show initiative

7. positive

8. enthusiastic

9. open-minded

10. dedicated

Having a sense of humor and being creative may also come in handy.

Remember, be gently relentless!

Chapter 8

Technophobia!
Maria Fong's Story

"**W**hat the heck is a hard drive?" wondered Maria Fong, echoing the sentiments of many middle-aged computer-phobic people. Her technical knowledge of the computer was to turn it on, click an icon, and get into the Internet. Yet, it fascinated her. Now she cannot live without her computer. "We are attached. I can't be without it." Maria is a proud graduate with honors of a diploma in Business Information Systems. How did she go from fear to finesse?

Maria was born in Portugal and lived in France. She had to learn English at the age of 18 when she came to Canada. She was a stay-at-home mom for 11 years and looked after her ailing mother daily. At home, she felt she had "lost herself along the way." She thought she was only good at being a mom. Self-confidence eluded her. She took a correspondence writing course in children's literature. She did not believe her stories were good enough, in spite of her teachers' compliments. "It was not so much fear of rejection, but a fear that they weren't really good enough," she explained.

Maria earned her diploma in two years. Nevertheless, she was embarrassed that her young sons had to show her how to save files on her computer. Her friend dragged her to a local college in January 2001 and insisted she sign up for 'Computers 101' or they would not leave. She was still homemaking and looking after her mother. Reluctantly she signed on. "I was so afraid of messing up—of erasing the whole computer," she recalls. Yet, after just a few sessions, she was in love with that technological wonder. She not only learned like a sponge, she wanted to know what made the computer tick on the inside. Her loyal friend encouraged her to get a certificate as a Micro Computer Programmer. She envisioned "little nerdy people writing code. Did I ever find out that it was so different!" she laughs.

Now, moving like a steamroller, Maria was always studying, taking course after course. Imagine her surprise at getting 99 percent on her math test, considering that she had not taken math in 20 years and had hated it in her high school days when she barely got a passing grade in the subject. Her greatest feat was putting her computer back together in better working order than before, when it crashed.

You can go all the way to diploma, insisted her cheerleader. And so, she did. She felt twinges of guilt about neglecting her children, but they never mentioned a word. She feels that they see her hard-earned success as a positive example. When her mom died a year after she started the computer course, although she was sad, some of her burden eased. Initially, her husband did not think her choice of field was appropriate. Impressed when she reconfigured her computer, he asked her to reinstall his operating system. He now regularly asks her for computer advice.

Tears of joy and frustration dotted Maria's year's of achievements. "This stage is harder than 20 years ago, with kids, burdens of life, and other demands. But, I have had so many wonderful experiences and growth. I will feel that I have truly succeeded when I am actually teaching what I learned. To transfer that knowledge to someone else, I know, will have a major impact.

Maria-Jose Fong, Richmond Hill, Ontario. Marijo4711@yahoo.com

Computer Help for the Uninitiated

I make my living from using the computer but I find it a frustrating, exhausting process. Internet searches drive me batty. I have to go very deep into links to actually find what I want. If I type in 'skilled trades for women' in Yahoo, I get listings of 'fragrances for women.' Apparently, there is no distinguishing between topics, as long as it contains the word 'women.' Google™ is more discriminating in laying out its topics. I often waste hours looking up something that should be so simple.

Love it or hate it, Bill Gates and others in the industry rule our world. The computer is here to stay. There are virtually no jobs left that you do not have to have at least some basic computer skills for, whether related to communication, research or reporting. Applications for jobs are often completed via computer.

So what is a technophobe to do? Opt to get on-line, even if you have to invest some time and money. Obtaining a personal computer is paramount to employment survival.

There are government- and community-sponsored programs that offer basic computer training. They are usually inexpensive and some-times free (be cautious here; it could be legitimate, but sometimes there are hidden costs). They are frequently self-taught, meaning that you are given an instruction book, which you follow at your own pace, increasing your level of skill. A facilitator may be available to answer questions, but be prepared to wait for help if there are many students in the class. This may not be the most optimal way to learn. Learning happens in various modes and if your style is not by reading a book, you may be lost. You can also learn on-line. Type in 'on-line basic computer training.' Ask your local librarian to recommend a course. *See Resources section at the end of this book.*

Alternatively, there are many colleges and universities that offer pro-fessional courses. If you require funding for courses, check your local employment service center to see how you can apply for financial assistance.

The following, which I wrote in poem format, summarizes my parting thoughts on the subject of computers!

Computer Woes

When computers are good,
they are really great.
But, when they are bad,
I become sooooo irate.

As a writer
in this techie age,
clearing spam,
puts me in a rage.

There are so many things
lost in cyberspace,
it's a cryin' shame
and an awful waste.

When I used a paper
and a pen,
my state of mind
was much more Zen.

Pop-up boxes,
viruses too,
drive me mad
and make be blue.

I delete the same messages
over and over again.
I'm surprised I haven't ended up
in the loony bin.

I use more paper
than ever before.
I'm a glutton for punishment,
cuz I keep printing more.

Maybe the Aboriginals
got it right:
their stories were oral,
they did not write.

There was no downloading,
nor passwords either.
Life was simpler,
trapping beaver.

They bonded with
the oral word.
There was no such thing
as a computer nerd.

For what we've gained,
we've lost much more.
We are automatons
to the core.

Chapter 9

Dress for Success

Hopefully you are past the 'hippy, grunge, punk, gothic, rapper' looks that defined each of the last four decades. In the job market, conservative and well-groomed is the name of the game. You can be comfortable by putting a little spunk into your attire. Feeling good and looking good will be the ticket to your success.

If I believe in a product that has benefited me, I think that others should benefit also. There is a line of clothing—a stretchy, slinky material (an acetate/spandex knit)—that is not only comfortable, but looks fabulous on most people. It is made by the Canadian company Picadilly Fashions and has distributors in the US. Compared to a wool suit, the prices are considerably less. You can buy four or five pieces, often for the price of one traditional business suit.

Because the material is weightier than similarly made materials, it has a lovely drape on the body, so is flattering, no matter what your size. The waists are elastic. They have a velvety sheen to them. They wash and wear beautifully, so you save on dry-cleaning costs and you help the environment.

Choose classic colors suitable for interviews, including black and navy. You can purchase these as pantsuits or skirt suits with co-coordinating tops of different colors. You can add pieces for more formal wear. It is perfect for travel because it does not wrinkle.

Buying a few pieces that mix and match makes for a cost-effective, long-lasting, classic and easy-care wardrobe. I have been wearing these clothes for the past 10 years. I own almost every color and several styles. I get many compliments.

If money is an issue, there are non-profit organizations that provide gently used or new suits and other garments suitable for interviews for women at a small cost or for free. All clothing is carefully cleaned and mended, if necessary. An excellent program for this purpose and to help women get jobs, retain their jobs and succeed in the mainstream marketplace is Dress for Success. To access services, it requires that the woman be referred by a non-profit or government agency. Each client will receive a suit when she has a job interview and then another suit if she gets the job.

Suppose there is no affiliate Dress for Success near you. This could be an opportunity to start a career in fashion and help other women. Dress for Success will help you to establish a program. Or consider starting a clothing exchange in your community.

To be sure what clothing you will require for an interview, check Resources at the end of this book for professional advice. The Washington State University Web site provides specific advice on what to wear, including samples with comments on whether it is appropriate.

For other sources for inexpensive (or free—check with each agency) clothing or to find out where you can go, check out:

- Goodwill Industries;
- United Way;
- Salvation Army;
- Local religious institutions;
- Local non-profit or government agencies.

Chapter 10

Emerging From the Underworld
Laurie Palmer's Story

Laurie Palmer's feet kept slipping and sliding from the mud-encrusted walls as she desperately tried to claw her way up from the deep, dark, dank ditch. When she finally reached the top and crawled out, she washed the mud off, but the scars from the battering will remain forever. Her battle scars have become her 'mantra to the world.'

"I was released from prison October of 1993. I have never been back since. In February of 2004, I was awarded a Woman of Triumph award for overcoming my trials and helping other women. I had to go through this journey for me to fulfill my life purpose of helping other broken women. If I could do it, so can you."

Laurie's story is a powerful testament to the strength of the human spirit. She was born when her mother was the tender age of 15—a child having a child. Dysfunction surrounded Laurie and her four siblings from the beginning. Her parents lived a tormented lifestyle in a black ghetto in Portland, Oregon, that was rampant in drugs, drinking, whoring and crime. As early as eight years old, Laurie knew that life was not normal. "My life revolved around people who were drug dealers, addicts, pimps, prostitutes, shoplifters. I remember saying that when I grow up I will not be like these people. I will never use drugs."

Her only experience with church was being picked up every Sunday by bus and taken to a "white church." Laurie's mother taught her to "never trust white people." Therefore, Laurie eyed her faith healers with suspicion. She soon realized that they meant no harm. "These people showed me nothing but love and taught me the love of God." A seed was planted in Laurie that would help her many years later during the darkest period of her life.

Saying something is one thing, following through is another. Her churchgoing and awareness of the sordid life that surrounded her did not prevent Laurie from falling into a life of disrepair. By the age of 12, she experienced her first encounter with marijuana. "Wow, this is cool," she thought. The drug made her more self-conscious. She swiftly expanded her life-altering chemical of choice to alcohol. Alcohol made her the person she yearned to be—no longer shy, and now fitting in with her peers. Laurie was like a "lost child" trying to find her way back home.

As she got older, Laurie did more serious drugs, including cocaine and heroin. She was really striving, grasping for love and acceptance. "I grew up not knowing emotions, except as a child I remember feeling ugly and unloved. My mother was a single mom. I came from a home where you spoke only when spoken to and had to obey commands of 'clean up' and 'look after your brother,' since I was the oldest." As a teenager, the years of neglect and abuse validated her negativity and she projected exactly what she had been told she was: lazy and useless. It became a Catch-22. The more she reached out for love and acceptance, the more trouble she got into.

Her young teen years were plagued with abortions, running away from home, prostituting and crime. She eased her way into the dark world of corruption by shoplifting, "so I could dress nice like everybody else." Her shoplifting progressed to stealing a purse from a store employee. The wallet held a Visa card, which Laurie saw fit to use at her disposal, buying a pair of shoes for her boyfriend. "The police were called and I was charged with my first felony. This was the beginning of a long criminal lifestyle. You name it, I had done it." Felony would be a word that would haunt Laurie for years to come.

She became a ward of the court. Home for the next 15 years was juve-
nile detention centers and prisons.

At Hillcrest, a lock-up institution for girls, Laurie was first exposed to
what emotions meant. "The counselor told me while I was in a group
of girls, that I wore my emotions on my sleeve. 'What are you talking
about? What are emotions?' I had no clue what was being said to me.
After the explanation, suddenly titles and names could be attached to
my feelings. I understood that if I am angry and just burst out, that it
has an effect on other people. The seed of knowledge was planted, but
it takes awhile for that seed to grow. Harvesting comes later. It was not
the magic key. I had a better understanding of my feelings. I would
sometimes analyze my behavior, but I still didn't know how to fix it."

Eighteen years old and Laurie was the mother of two children from
different fathers. "I stayed home with my children all day and went to
work on the streets at night. I thought I was living a normal life, until
I ended up losing my children to the state. Even that didn't stop me."

Twelve more years would pass before Laurie could put a halt to her
death-defying life.

Her addiction to alcohol was "out of control" and her criminal activities were becoming more violent, including "stabbing her 'tricks' when
they got out of line." Her worst crime was running over two women
and dragging a man with her car because they had jumped her. "I
remember planning the whole thing. I wanted them dead. I had been
drinking all day. The police watched the whole incident from across
the street. All I remember is flashing lights, taking them on a high-
speed chase that ended with police guns drawn and screaming for me
to put my hands above my head and get out of the car or they would
shoot. It was like being in a dream." No one died. Laurie was convicted of assault with a deadly weapon and not attempted murder.

Back in prison, for the umpteenth time, Laurie reunited herself with
her faith. The fact that her victims did not die and she had received a
lesser conviction, she believed, was because of "Divine intervention."

She signed up for "every self-help class the prison had to offer" and began to attend the prison church, "seeking God." It was there that she met Fran, the Bible teacher brought in from an outside ministry. Laurie felt comfortable with Fran, who was always nice. Laurie related her sordid life tale, moving Fran to tears. Fran vowed never to let Laurie down, saying that she would be there for her. She gave Laurie her book *Lord Heal My Hurts*, by Kay Arthur. It turned out to be Laurie's "saving grace." She began to understand things that were alien to her previously. Yet, sadly, Laurie was not yet destined to be on a path of righteousness.

Prison, although meant as a deterrent and rehabilitation institution, does not always fulfill its goals. Pent-up anger and frustration among inmates often goes unchecked. Hardened criminals learn innovative tricks to do other kinds of crimes underneath the noses of the guards. Guards either turn a blind eye or are helpless to stop the manipulation and control. Laurie tells of "learning stuff" she didn't know—stuff that included forgery and bribery. Laurie was fearful the first time she went to prison, having heard horror stories of gang rapes, murder, lesbianism, assaults. It did not take long for her to learn the ropes and integrate into the prison community. Laurie's final act of aggression before her road to recovery began happened 13 years after her first incarceration.

After beating someone up for calling her the "N word," she received nine months in isolation. It was the first time Laurie had ever been completely alone for an extended period of time. With nothing else to do, she started to take stock of her life. "I was tired and I knew it would not be long before I was dead or killed someone. My children were wards of the state and I thought I had lost my rights." Reaching out to her spiritual needs, she wrote the prison chaplain asking for a Bible and prayer. He came to her, said a prayer and left her with a Bible. The Bible, written as it is, was hard for her to understand, so she gave up.

An envelope arrived one day containing a picture of her smiling children dressed up. Her first reaction was happiness, but it quickly turned to sadness. There was a woman in the picture with her children. "Who does she think she is, acting like my kids' mom?" Laurie thought, hurt and angry. However, the answer came from within her: "Look at you, a drug addict sitting in a cell. I started to cry out to the Lord. I picked up my Bible and flipped through the pages, daring God to speak to me in the midst of my situation. I flipped one page and I couldn't understand it. I cried out to God one more time and flipped to Psalm 20 (A Prayer for Victory). He said, 'I hear thee in a time of trouble.' I lost it. I repented and cried out so loud that the officer came running to my cell asking me what was wrong. I told her that I was crying out to God. They left me alone. I had never felt as good as I felt on that day." It was the beginning of a new life.

In 1992, while still in prison, Laurie participated in an in-patient alcohol and drug program called Turning Point. Asserting her dreams that she would one day help other women who had followed the same path, Laurie was not taken seriously. They saw her as intimidating and wrote her off because of her background and limited education—a rather odd position, Laurie felt, for a program designed to help women turn their lives around.

Nine months into the program, Laurie found herself terminated from the treatment program and sent back to the general prison population. Wanting to use up the remaining seven months of her sentence wisely, she walked by a window in general population, saw a class of women, and inquired what they were doing. She was told it was called WICS (Women in Community Service). It was a pilot project being tested out in a prison setting. Regular women from the community came in to share life skills with women in prison to help them transition back into their community with survival tools. Laurie kicked up a fuss and was accepted into the program. (Now this program is offered to most inmates.) Laurie was given her own mentor— a woman who is still her friend today and, in fact, sang at Laurie's wedding. The program helped Laurie land her first real job on day-work release while she finished off her sentence.

"I was scared at the interview. I felt that I had FELON stamped across my forehead," she recalls of the emotion that is universal—fear. Nevertheless, she was determined to get the job. She wanted to get her children back. She had never experienced a normal life—now it was her vision. She was taught how to turn the negative into the positive and how to respond when the fated question arose, "I see here that you have a criminal record. What was your crime?" With eloquent skill and using the tools she now had, Laurie calmly told her interviewer that her crime was in the past and was not who she was at present. She showed him the WICS certificate and told him of her remorse. She spoke of her two children who needed a mother to support them. It was obvious that the man, dressed like a cowboy, really cared and wanted to give her a chance. Laurie got the job as cleaner in a food court of a mall. She worked herself up over three years to become supervisor and got a good letter of reference when she left. What was more important, Laurie got her children back.

After Lifeskills™ and out of prison, Laurie continued working at the food court until Laurie's cousin, who was in the same aftercare program Laurie had just completed, ran into some issues. Laurie went to advocate for her. The director of the program saw Laurie's potential first-hand. He asked her if she had ever thought about being an alcohol and drug counselor. "We are short African-American counselors and you will make a good one." He offered to put her through state training that they would pay. Elated at the prospect that she would finally be able to serve her life's purpose, she talked to her husband and agreed to take the position. One day while working, she decided to pull her file that had been forwarded from the Turning Point program. She opened her file and was dismayed to find that the woman from Turning Point had written: *Laurie has the idea that she would one day be an alcohol and drug counselor. We don't feel she has the education or skills to do that.* It was the fuel that started the fire.

"I felt empowered, needed, valuable. I could offer my past experiences and be a role model." Women tell her constantly, "You are an inspiration. You motivated me. You are the reason I changed. If you can do it, I can do it. I need your support…"

Laurie has evolved and grown in the social service industry over the past decade. She has just completed a three-year grant position and is taking a bit of a breather. Laurie recently completed a career change assistance program that assessed her, and now motivational speaking features prominently in Laurie's future. That is her dream. She is already speaking about her life for programs like WICS, and on radio and television programs. "It is a calling to speak to people's hearts and to what is meaningful. By helping others figure out where to go in their life, I am helping myself," she says passionately and without bitterness. "The process has been like a baby learning to walk. They fall, but they pick themselves back up. Eventually they will run."

Laurie warns that the road ahead, when coming from the underbelly of life, is not easy and certainly not perfect. Sometimes there are relapses. Knowledge is power, so the more you learn, the better you can deal with problems. "I knew I could live differently. That there was a better life for me out there. I began to change my mental attitude and then to live up to my thinking. Once I did that and stepped out on faith, I was able to walk into that belief."

From one who has been "down and dirty" with life, take Laurie's advice: "The first principal of achievement is mental attitude. People begin to achieve when they begin to believe."

Laurie Palmer, 42, Portland, Oregon.

This contribution, ©2005-2006, is used with permission.

Laurie Palmer received the Woman of Triumph award, from Women Work! The National Network for Women's Employment, Washington, DC. www.womenwork.org 1-202-467-6346 fax 1-202-467-5366 America Works Because Women Work!®

Chapter 11

How to De-stress About Stress

Let's face it, looking for a job, switching careers or going into your own business is stressful. As if life is not stressful enough, we find ourselves stressed as our worrying expands out of proportion.

For me, trying to get this book done on deadline meant not going to the gym as often, which meant more stress. I am already the queen of "no sweat." I've always hated to sweat, but my body hasn't figured that out yet because every hour I am drenched. It must be the "Menoclaws." Nevertheless, I regularly trudge off to my local Women's Fitness Club of Canada, wearing my colorful, coordinated socks and T-shirt, where I am able to de-stress because I can:

- look like I just got rolled over by a truck;
- be overweight;
- not have to arrange my cleavage (the little that I have) to heave over the top of my bra;
- or wear dental-floss outfits up my rear for the benefit of male oglers.

Sometimes, forgetting to eat was also a problem. No positive result there—the weight still did not melt away because I was just sitting all day. Sleep was rare; I'd wake up every hour, it seemed, sweating of course, my mind racing like a computer, 'young' adult children coming in and going to bed late... So who am I to tell you how to deal with stress?

Well, I have discovered little things that can be done daily while you are doing what you normally do. Instead of telling you what all the stress experts are telling you, including eat well, sleep more, exercise, avoid stressful situations (you would have to avoid life)—things we all know anyway—my tips that follow are doable and may even be enjoyable.

1. Sit on a bouncing ball. There are not many of us who are not couch- or computer-potatoes. Sit on a 55 cm exercise ball. They are inexpensive and you can get them at any fitness store. You need a pump also to keep it inflated. Guaranteed, you will not fall asleep. It will force your posture straight, and if you so desire you can start bouncing. Strange but fun. If your whole family did it together, what a hoot. Be careful you do not fall off, though. I did. I backed the ball into a hanging file folder in my office (a room that is getting smaller and smaller), the ball burst and I crashed to the floor. I now have a six-inch scar on my arm where it dragged along the metal corner of the folder. My bum was sore for a while after, too!

2. Pop in your favorite CD or tape (if your machine can still play them) in a player or listen to your favorite music station on the radio while cooking or cleaning. For great benefit, do an Ellen DeGeneres-type dance to the fridge or stove, or while you vacuum. For a great belly chuckle and sage life advice, buy Loretta LaRoche's (the "Master of Mirth") CDs. She is an international stress-management consultant who pokes fun at all of life's quirks and quacks. She also has DVDs which are hysterical to watch.

3. Instead of meeting your friends for coffee, have them come to your house and exercise to a rollicking Richard Simmons DVD or organize a belly-dancing session. You can have your coffee afterwards.

4. When it rains, use a funny umbrella. Mine belonged to my daughter and is a hot pink 'Bugs Bunny' (the ears stand by themselves!). And do not forget to splash in the puddles.

5. Try to learn an interesting or fun new thing every day by talking to a colleague, family member or friend.

6. Compliment somebody everyday. Making someone else feel good will make *you* feel good.

7. Smile a lot and find the humor in life.

8. If e-mails, computers, televisions and telephones are driving you mad, make a No Information Technology Zone (NITZ). This one takes a lot of will power. My Saturdays and Sundays are e-mail free, meaning I do not check my messages. Sure, Monday mornings are a nuisance while I clear 45 e-mails, most of them telling me how I can be the best man I can for my woman, but at least I've had two days of not having to think about Viagra!

9. Make the shower or bath as hot as you can tolerate it, before you go to bed. If you are into using aromatherapy (essential oils from plants that promote psychological well-being—check with a health food store or pharmacy; you heat these in a special diffuser or burn them as candles, lighting them just as you are entering the shower/bath), the combined heat and scents help to relax your muscles and mind. **Make sure you check with your doctor regarding any aromatic oils that could affect your health.** Please sing (or hum quietly) in the shower.

10. Read an inspirational book at bedtime instead of watching the news.

11. Try taking a free on-line stress test by typing in 'Free Stress Tests.'

Chapter 12

Turning a Shopping Habit Into a Career
Sharon Edwards' Story

Shopaholics listen up. Your fetish may be the key to a lucrative, passionate career!

Sharon Edwards was not quite a full-fledged shopaholic, but nonetheless, she loved shopping. As a working woman, she wanted to maintain a certain image with her clothes. Her outfits were crafted with great care. "Shopping was a means to be creative," Sharon says, reflecting on her past life as a medical assistant in a clinic.

Sharon had been a 'jill'-of-all trades for 14 years in her previous life. She did everything from secretarial work, to doing blood work and the books for the clinic. The latter is something she still does for the clinic two times a month, but on her terms. Year 12 of that life left her restless, "but I didn't have the courage to make a change. I knew I was becoming invisible to myself. I wanted to be my own person." She does not deny that while raising her children (she was a stay-at-home mom for 13 years until her youngest son of three children went to school full-time) the part-time job was both convenient and afforded her a good lifestyle. Nevertheless, she was stuck in a rut with no capacity to grow.

Seeking independence, Sharon wanted to be self-employed. "I didn't want to watch the clock or answer to anyone. I wanted to be creative and to make my own mistakes without it affecting anyone else," she avowed. Her dream to break free simmered and stewed for two more years. When her children's lives changed with marriages and moving out, Sharon was ready to evolve—although to what she had no clue.

Many great ideas have percolated from a group sitting around a table drinking coffee. More brains are better than one. Sharon sat with a group of female friends discussing the woes of menopause. Only Sharon and one other woman had achieved that rite of passage. The others were merely beginning their journey. They talked about the symptoms: hot flashes where water became a desperate need, too many "senior moments" when memory was non-existent, and so on. "We should develop a menopause survival kit" was the brilliant suggestion. It had to be fun. It would not be about supplements. Sharon and her soon-to-be business partner ran with the idea.

Sharon did her homework, discussed the idea with her family who were supportive and decided it was a risk worth taking. The name was registered and a bank account opened. Sharon's employer was dismayed upon hearing of her decision to leave. Sharon had been a key person in their organization. However, they were supportive and recognized, given the kind of person she was, that it was bound to happen.

It took six months of extensive research, talking to business people about what a home business required—insurance, legalities, supplies, resource products, hooking up with the Canadian Federation of Independent Business and attending the Canadian Gift and Trade Association gift shows—before the business opened. There never was a formal business plan created, because she invested her own money and did not borrow from a bank. Sharon had gone from a salary and stability to no income, except for her husband's, and "a lot of self-doubt and fear."

"I began second-guessing my decision. People would be coming into my home. Would they be receptive? My days had been cut out for me while I was employed. My life had structure. Suddenly my time was my own, which I wanted but I did not know what I would do to fill my day. I needed to feel that I was accomplishing and contributing. I felt guilty that I was not bringing in money. Even with my plan, things did not always go that way. The loneliness enveloped me. Many times I thought I should go back to work, but I knew I couldn't." So she kept on plugging along.

Menopause Power—(with the slogan "Take the time to pause and pamper yourself") started with few items—tea pots and mugs, soothing teas, small fans, water bottles and hand towels imprinted with her logo, aromatherapy and journals for the forgetful—all packaged simply but attractively in corrugated boxing or cellophane. The items were sold individually also. The launch of the business was celebrated with a wine and cheese get-together for family and friends. The product line was set up in a small room in Sharon's house. The response was "amazing. It gave me the confidence to know that I was headed in the right direction," she says, oozing self-assurance. Effective networking started to snowball. What surprised Sharon was that the menopause things were not moving as she had anticipated. The fans were a novelty at first, but there was more interest in the mugs and teapots.

An astute observer, Sharon quickly keyed into what her customers wanted. She changed the focus to unique giftware, laid out more money and moved her showroom to the basement (recently vacated by her youngest son). She altered the name to **Pause Power—Unique Giftwear for Women** (eventually dropping women, so as to not limit her customer base). She is still reinvesting money made back into the business because she believes it is viable and will pay for itself soon.

A chance to participate in a vendors' show brought new prospects and opened up the door to women's business networking groups. For Sharon, it exposed a world she did not know existed. The stories, support, encouragement and dynamics provided her with the confidence that she could do it. It validated the direction she had taken. As she attended more women's networking events and meetings, many of her insecurities began to melt away.

"I know I made the right choice by leaving my job and becoming my own boss. The freedom to make my own decisions, work according to my own schedule and have flexibility, has allowed me to balance my life better. This choice has also forced me to reach out and learn so much more about myself. I have the confidence to pursue my dreams, although I don't always know what those dreams are. What I am realizing is that I am capable of doing anything I want to and if one thing does not work out, something else will. One idea leads to a hundred others, and with determination, hard work and effort, I can make things happen. I am learning from my mistakes and I listen very carefully to the experiences of other women to help guide me along my journey." Doubts sometimes still hover in the shadow, but Sharon is no longer afraid of the curves in the road and she is content not to be an overachiever.

Sharon's 10 tips for the new woman entrepreneur:

1. Strive for balance. Decide what you expect out of life before making a commitment. Be careful not to be so consumed with every detail of your business that it affects other aspects of your life. Make time for yourself, family and friends. [Sharon does not want to work as hard in the next fifty years as she did the first fifty! She learned it is okay not to have something to do every minute of the day.]

2. Say no when you have to.

3. Start small, taking baby steps. If you are buying inventory, do not buy more than you can afford or that you anticipate you will sell.

4. Make sure the name of your company reflects what you do. Sharon has once again renamed to **Sharon's Shop at Home— Unique Giftware.**

5. Have patience.

6. Learn about the computer (which was daunting for her).

7. Set up a Web site (that is on Sharon's to-do list).

8. Connect with other women for ideas, support and possible collaboration.

9. Be passionate about your product or service.
10. Try not to dwell on self-doubt—keep one foot in front of the other.

By the way, Sharon no longer has a burning desire to shop for herself. Her showroom organization and lovely packaging of her products has fulfilled her personal shopping need!

Sharon Edwards, Thornhill, Ontario.

This contribution, ©2005-2006, is used with permission.

To buy the gift that will get a "WOW" when you present it, visit **Sharon's Shop at Home —Unique Giftware** by appointment only at 1-647-298-0112, fax 1-905-886-2477, e-mail rosh_ent@hotmail.com.

If shopping is your bag, consider some of the following careers:

* Mystery shoppers get paid to shop by a company to see if service, selection and quality are good. Often you get to keep the purchases, as well. Personal shoppers go shopping for others who do not have the time, patience or skill to shop. Purchases can range from gifts to groceries. *See Resources section.*

* Buyer—This is a position that either you work your way up to or that you have to take university/college courses for. This should not stop you from approaching a place that may need a buyer if you can convince them that you have the knowledge and skills to do the job. The worst that can happen is that they say no.

* Consider opening up a store with merchandise that interests you. Again, this is a business venture and should be treated seriously.

* Writing for Shopping Guides—Find out what the criteria are or start your own publication.

* Writing a shopping column or tips for a newspaper, on-line, radio or television.

* Find out about opportunities with television shopping shows.

Chapter 13

Losing a Life Partner
Diane Sawyer's Story

Life can be cruel. Sometimes it can kick you in the gut, leaving you gasping for air and wondering how you are going to survive. Yet, the human spirit can surprise with resiliency—a strength that you never knew was buried so deep within. In times of need, that power rises to the surface, keeping you grounded.

When Diane Sawyer lost her "best friend, soul mate and financial provider"—her husband of 20 years—she discovered that life would go on, albeit differently. "I was 49, too young to be wearing black all my life," she asserted. She dug in her heels to prove to her detractors that she could make her life successful on her own.

Diane had a privileged life with her second husband, Al. He was a special man. They met while she was living in Calgary, having just been divorced. Her new beau would even pay the babysitting, and included her two young daughters from her previous marriage in their activities as though they were his own. When he went back to his home in Toronto and offered Diane "a life," it was an offer she could not refuse.

Al presented Diane with an upscale lifestyle. He was partner in a family printing business, but his passion was buying, restoring and collecting antique cars. World travel and fine dining were now part of Diane's life. The couple purchased a magnificent 12-acre property out in the country with hills, a pond and a lovely home.

Al wanted Diane to be his business partner, assisting in his successful printing business and accompanying him when pursuing his passion for antique cars. She happily obliged him, only working part-time as a legal secretary. "Chasing cars," as she calls it, is still something she pursues with relish.

Her wonderful life came to a screeching halt, when on one of their usual jaunts to the US in April of 1998, a tragedy occurred. In was a Sunday in Carlisle, Pennsylvania, home to one of the largest car shows in the world. Al had made a car purchase the day before. He was anxious to pick up his prize from the owner, and was upset that the man was unavailable to meet early that day. To kill some time, he and Diane decided to go for a breakfast with some friends. Breakfast that day was one of those large buffets where eating in abundance is all too easy. Although Al was muscular, he was certainly not obese. Al did live with angina, however. His doctor had told him that if he were to be doing anything physical, to not eat before and to not lift anything more than 10 pounds. In between eating that particular morning, he was nervously getting up every 20 minutes to call the car seller. Finally, they found him at home, and they were able to go pick up the car.

Many times when Al and Diane traveled to these shows, they did so with a convoy. This time they had with them their new pickup truck, with a camper attached and a hitched trailer hauling an antique car. Diane and Al were driving the pickup. Trailing behind were some friends in other newly acquired cars, including a 1960 Chevrolet convertible (Diane still owns it). Al was restless about wanting to keep moving, deciding not to stop at a particular red light. That would have been dangerous enough had there been traffic on the road, but that was not the fate awaiting him. His friends behind were reluctant to break the law and did stop. Consequently, Al had to pull over to wait for them to catch up.

The red light proved to be fatal for an unexpected reason. The old Chevy stalled at the red light. Al jumped out of his truck, went to push the stalled car, and collapsed. After the initial shock to everyone present and with uncertainty about what exactly had happened, Diane moved the rig Al had parked in a rush, off the main road into a lot. Simultaneously, she called 911.

"It was a comedy of errors," she reels at the memory, still fresh in her mind. "Everything he wasn't supposed to do, he did: the big meal, the anxiety. He was a man of no vices, except that he had an A-type personality—always rushing, always having to be productive. He also was not a joker. I knew it was serious when he went down. After parking the rig, I ran back to help, trying to resuscitate him, having recently taken a CPR course. The ambulance arrived. At the hospital, he was pronounced dead on arrival. It was surreal."

Al was Jewish, and according to Jewish law, the body should be buried intact, with no donation of organs. That law is not definitive. Some rabbinical authorities believe it is considered a "mitzvah" or good deed that you are giving someone else life. It mattered little to Diane who was not Jewish. They had a friend who had had a kidney transplant and was doing well and another friend who was looking for donor eyes because he was going blind. When the doctors asked for her permission to use Al's organs to help someone else, her response was an automatic "yes."

Her decision caused a rift between her and his family, but she knew she had made the right decision. The day Al was buried, she received a call from an administrator at the Hershey Medical Center in Pennsylvania that two people were seeing because of Al. "I think that he would have felt good knowing that his final act was to help someone else. It was a blessing to me also," she says thoughtfully, knowing that her dear husband had contributed to the quality of others' lives.

Traumatized by the sudden death of the man she had loved and respected, she reacted on adrenalin that night. Friends and family members offered to fly to Pennsylvania to get her and drive the truck and the cars back home. She declined their offer. Her acceptance that her husband and best friend was not coming home with her was swift. The hospital had to arrange for him to be sent home for burial on Wednesday. Although "it was tough leaving him there," Diane made a decision that she needed "to take control." She drove the truck with a friend of her husband's for four hours until they hit bad weather and the friend took over. The normal eight-hour ride turned into 13 hours because they got lost. Tears flowed from the bereaved drivers.

Death and critical illness often bring out the worst in people. Greed can enter into the picture, and there are those who think that the best course of action for a "dependant" wife is to sell the house and pack it all in. Diane loved her house, the camper and the cars. She was not going to let others tell her that that way of life was unacceptable. "If I sold my house, bought a condo and had a fortune in the bank, what would I do? Who would I be?" Diane found out who her true friends were. In time, she cut off relations with her husband's family, who were relentlessly critical. Some friends of her husband tried to take advantage of the fact she was a woman in a man's world and sought to buy the couple's cars and parts well below market value. A close friend of Al's took charge of that department, keeping her away from the vultures.

Her own supportive family and friends helped her heal "that sad summer." Her youngest daughter, her daughter's husband and child, Samantha, born on the same day as Al, moved in with her. Her brother from Calgary came to stay and never left Toronto. She celebrated her 50th birthday, with a party her daughter Debbie and several close friends gave for her. It was bittersweet. The fact remained, she was a widow. "I wasn't supposed to turn 50 by myself," she bemoans of her great loss. "Even when loved ones surround me, I can still feel alone." In spite of it, she was ready to move on. She volunteered at a hospital.

Regardless of their lifestyle, Al had not left her with a fortune, and when the two-year mark arrived, Diane decided she needed money.

A former employer of an insurance company asked her to work for him on a part-time basis. Within a few months, her oldest daughter, Donna, became ill in Calgary. Diane rushed to her daughter's side. The event made Diane realize that she wanted freedom to look after her family at critical times, and also to camp with her granddaughter and enjoy her grandchildren out west, maintain her house and continue to travel. The idea of working for herself now became entrenched in her mind.

Diane was introduced to multi-level sales for a telecommunications company. She knew enough about the business to know that it had potential to be profitable and that it offered good customer service. She plunged herself into that world as an independent representative, traveling, meeting people and loving every minute of it. When things changed in company policy, Diane decided to move in another direction as well. She is now also an independent representative for a major health and wellness company. "It's all about helping people find quality in their lives. It is what I love."

The pain of her grief still revisits often. "When a radio contest offers a trip for two, I don't think to enter. Who would I take?" she wonders aloud. "Or when I go to a car show alone, I rarely go out to eat at a nice restaurant. I have been unable to find somebody yet who has the same interests, the same passions and who can offer me the lifestyle and security my Al gave me. People tell you to get on with your life, but it is harder to do as a widow. And I have found advantages to being single—something I would never have believed. There are many sad relationships out there." Diane does not wallow in self-pity; instead, she chooses to enjoy the gifts of her family, close friends and her career.

Seven years after the death of her beloved husband, Diane is proud of the fact that she is still in the house she adores. She is the only woman that she is aware of who packs auto parts to sell at automotive flea markets. After 25 years, cars continue to thrill her. People at the shows still talk fondly of her kind-hearted, honest, knowledgeable husband. Their comments touch her soul with pleasure. She eagerly anticipates challenges and looks to her accomplishments for strength.

Diane advises women who have gone through a death of a spouse "to not ever give up, don't sell your house and move, don't change careers, and be careful not to start a new relationship too soon. Wait a year to give yourself time to heal. Find something you will really love and be passionate about it. Inner strength can become your greatest asset."

Diane Sawyer, 56, Kleinburg, Ontario.

This contribution, ©2005-2006, is used with permission.

Let Diane share her joy with you. Contact her at www.shaklee.ca/ destindi e-mail destindi@myexcel.ca.

Chapter 14

Recovering From Addiction
Raven Crow's Story

Raven Crow loves bellies.

Raven is a master therapeutic belly dance instructor who incorporates creative and therapeutic exercises known as "ty belly fusion." "I was mesmerized by the control, movements and isolation," she says of the ancient art that changed her life. She chortles as she tells of her recent session with 400 Italian women, and how she got them to squat, letting them believe that it was part of the dance, only to tell them, "I was just kidding." The crowd laughed. A good thing, too—Raven's philosophy is that laughter is critical to good health.

It was 30 years ago that Raven signed up for belly dancing. "This lady was a godsend," Raven says gratefully of her instructor, Maria. Maria had escaped a Moroccan harem with her son. She was the first person who believed in Raven.

For six months, Raven "danced like a maniac, letting out hate and anger." She never uttered a word, nor did she mingle with the other women. One day, Raven's "savior" asked her if she would like to teach the class. Raven laughed out loud, but never spoke a word. The teacher took this to mean "yes" and put Raven's name in the calendar for the next session. Raven panicked, but her propelled her to stand in front of the class. "I stood up and faced those women," she states emphatically.

You see, Raven was an abused young woman, mentally and physically, including a gang rape by several male "friends." Drugs and alcohol ruled her days. She had tried to commit suicide at age 18. "I didn't really want to die," she reflects, and so was able to call her boyfriend who took her to the family doctor.

Nineteen and unmarried, she was pregnant. Her son, whom she considers her greatest gift, was born a day after her birthday. She admits that it was the first time she felt special. Belly dancing sustained her right up until the time she gave birth. Four weeks later, she bounced back teaching, doing this for the next eight years.

Her partner kept her clean and sober, and provided for her materially, but he was "a control freak." "I hated him with every fiber of my being, but it was a way to get out of my situation. I believed that you could learn to love somebody." She walked out of the relationship with no support, leaving her children behind. For 10 years after leaving, she "went to Hell and back." Her nasty habits of heavy drinking and drugs resumed.

At 27, she left Sudbury and stopped teaching belly dancing. She heard about a vocational rehabilitation program for adults in Oakville, but there were no openings. Threatening to attempt suicide if she had to wait, that evening they told her they had found a spot. She had 12 hours to pack. She was given a bus ticket, $100 to last the month, and the name and number of a doctor in Hamilton.

Exhausted and hungover, she arrived in Oakville. The Education Centre (a day facility) was locked. A $45 cab ride later (and that taken from the only $100 she had), they stopped in front of a rundown motel. Raven told the driver to wait; instead, he dumped her luggage and left. The motel was $55 a night. Hate and bad attitude overtook her as she told the clerk she could not afford it. She told her sordid story. He provided a musty room.

She called the doctor the next day, who told her to stay an extra night, which he paid for.

With a serious attitude problem, Raven appeared in her classroom the following morning. Her teacher, Kathy, asked the students if they knew of a place for her to stay. A male responded, saying his mom had a spare room. Kathy gave Raven her number in case of emergency.

For four hours (after school), Raven talked with the mom who offered her tea and coffee. Suddenly the mother blurted out "Get the f… out of my house, you're an Indian." It was Raven's first encounter with racism. Raven was not sure of her heritage at that time.

Raven called Kathy, who asked if Raven could get to her house. The son who had offered his house, along with his girlfriend, drove her to Kathy's large home. They watched as Raven made two trips to the house with all her luggage. She burst into tears when Kathy appeared. "I do not need this bull…I want to go home." The compassionate teacher told her it would be okay and took Raven in for several months.

Raven desperately tried to stay clean and sober. Kathy found another home for her that ended up being filthy. The owners were drug users. Raven found another place in Toronto. For two and a half hours each way, Raven commuted to her school in Oakville. During the whole nine-month course, she was never late.

Program representatives asked Raven many questions, trying to find out what made her tick. They discovered that she was gifted in visual merchandizing. She was sent to a fashion institute in Toronto, where she was kicked out because she failed everything except communications.

Raven harbored another secret: she was illiterate. As a young child in school, she had a cruel teacher (for two years, because she failed the first year) who would beat her on her hands. The sadistic woman beat the boy beside Raven from head to toe, pulled him up from his collar pointed her finger (Raven thought she was pointing at her), and threatened the others that if they did not listen it would happen to them. Raven could not hold a pen in her hand without "freaking out." paralyzed her ability to read and write.

Cut off from welfare and unable to hold a job, she was taken to a strip club by a man. He gave her a box and told her to dance. She refused, so he told her she would have to be a table dancer. She earned $50 for an eight-hour day. She was not a hustler and avoided dancing for $5 a song for individual men. Mostly, she would sit in the corner, shaking. She discovered that by being a feature or co-feature dancer, she only had to work 20-minute shows four or five times a day and get paid $750 a week. She bought a four-door Chevette, which she called home for three months.

Toronto clubs disliked her talent, so she went north of Barrie. She made up to $1650 a week, and never had contact with the men. She did not drink or do drugs. When she moved to North Bay, her evil spirits resurfaced. Breakfast consisted of a large mug half-filled with sambuca or other liqueur and the other half of vodka, 30 to 35 crushed codeine-laden Tylenol pills in water, a hit of acid and 20 joints. Amazingly, she still functioned. She became Killian Foster, because 'kill' fit her intense hatred and anger.

A "knight in shining armor" rescued her. For 12 years, he helped her get on the straight and narrow, but found fault with everything she did. She rekindled her love of teaching belly dancing for the Board of Education. "I pulled a Houdini on him; some nights when he thought I was teaching, I went to a school for abused women called L.A.M.P. (Lakeshore Area Multi-service Project). I would drive to different places, just in case he was following me." She learned to wean herself away from him, permanently.

• • •

Providence intervened, and Raven learned independence and gained confidence. Everyday, she would drop off a video and pass a local gym. She wanted to ask for a job but never did. A physical force dragged her into the gym, but nobody was there. A woman came from outside, explained details about the gym and handed her the schedule. It was closed on Thursdays. On impulse, Raven asked to rent the space, but was offered the whole basement. Rent was $400, which she paid out of the $600 she had managed to scrimp and save for eight years.

A month later, Raven opened her sunshine yellow "I Dream Belly Dancing" studio.

She connected with her aboriginal roots and found spiritual comfort in the belief that "The Creator looks after you. I believe I am a spiritual warrior." She has reunited with her children.

Her victory was learning to read at the age of 40. Simultaneously, she took a self-employment course where her "I Dream" plaque still graces the walls as the Women's Entrepreneur for the Year 1997.

Raven calls herself the "The Traveling Belly" because she spreads joy and heals bodies and souls throughout Greater Toronto. Her aboriginal friends have dubbed her The Red "O" as an honor—Red because of her native heritage and "O" because, like Oprah, she dispenses unconditional love, acceptance, generosity, wisdom and inspiration, while she teaches dancing.

"Today I feel like a newborn child. For the first time, I love my life. I've learned to trust that my Creator will guide me on her true destiny, not mine. I would not change one second of my life for it created who I am today!" Raven wishes everyone a "Belly, belly good day!"

Raven Crow, 51, Toronto, Ontario.

This contribution, ©2005-2006, is used with permission.

Raven Crow recently graduated from Miziwe Biik Aboriginal Employment and Training in Toronto www.miziwebiik.com, 416-591-2310. She has been featured in local and national media, including several television appearances. She is producing an instructional DVD and other media-related products. For private or group lessons, call 1-877-969-0109 toll-free, or in the Toronto area call 416-207-0350, www.idreamstudios.com.

Chapter 15

The Silver Fox of Comedy
Joyce Kaye's Story

"**A**ttention all women: There is no reason that you can't work like a man and have a career and a family. You just have to be wily enough to figure out how you can do both." So says Joyce Kaye— "homemaker, wife, mother, grandmother and retired from driving the kids to school. Now I drive them to their divorce lawyers!" This grandma does stand-up: "I don't mean physically getting up out of a chair, I am talking about stand-up comedy…a real live working comedienne."

Joyce had been "a kid in a candy store" (owned by her parents). Being an entertainer was a childhood dream. However, growing up in the late 1940s, early '50s in Brooklyn, in a working class family, being an entertainer was "not something that good girls should pursue." Her father called it "nonsense." So Joyce did what any dutiful child would do—at the age of 19 she married a good-looking musician.

Marriage at that age was appropriate back then. "It was the only way you could fool around," Joyce gleefully reminisces. It was "what good girls did." However, women were also supposed to be dutiful wives and be bound to the home. Their career was 'homemaking.' Joyce put her children and husband first, but she also extended her boundaries and created a career for herself.

Joyce's husband owned a music shop, while also attending university to get a music degree. Her two children ran around the store when they were quite young as Joyce managed the business on a part-time basis. She was also a musician. When the kids reached school age, Joyce arranged babysitting for them after school on certain days, in order to teach other kids piano and accordion. Her mother thwarted every opportunity for Joyce to succeed, including refusing to babysit her grandchildren, insisting that Joyce behave as a mother and be there for her kids. Her mother's reaction seemed rather ironic to Joyce, because her mother worked in the family candy store and still managed to raise her children as well. Perhaps her mother was guilt-ridden that she had had to work. In spite of her mother's feelings on the matter, Joyce continued to pursue her own interests.

As her children grew, so did Joyce's repertoire. She performed at weddings and other functions. But she ran smack dab into the feminist thought of the day that was advocating that women get out of the bedrooms and kitchens of the nation and into the boardrooms. Joyce viewed that as counterintuitive and held to the belief early on that, with planning and thought, it was possible to have both.

However, the new feminism was not the only issue.

A bigger obstacle was a strong anti-female stance (polarizing the feminist movement) pervading North America that women could not perform as equals in a man's world. Joyce's world of entertainment was included in that scenario. When she tried to get gigs herself, she was rejected because she was a woman. Being "on the ball," Joyce became Jackie Kaye (so named to parody President John F. Kennedy's wife Jackie) and registered herself with agencies, giving the impression to them that she was a man. Her ploy worked effectively.

While Joyce was playing the accordion at a Bar Mitzvah one Saturday afternoon, the hostess who had used an agency to hire the musician and was too busy with her guests to notice who her musician was, danced by Joyce and looked up, astounded to see that she was a woman. "You're not a man," sputtered the woman. "Not since the last time I checked," responded Joyce. "Is the music all right?"

Joyce asked. The woman nodded in agreement. "Do you want me to stop playing?" The woman shook her head and danced away, embarrassed. Joyce not only got a large tip that day, but the woman's friends took Joyce's card because it was so novel to have a female musician. She, who had posed to agencies as a he, went back to being a she!

While playing music paid the bills, Joyce wanted something more. "I have a big fat ego," she jokes. As a child, she had won awards as a comic and mimic. So at a women's luncheon one day, she started saying funny lines to catch their attention. It did the trick! People started hiring her to do a musical comedy shtick. Then they just hired her to be funny. A star was born. "I reinvented myself. I took the same thing and packaged it differently"—a theme Joyce has used for the last 30 years.

Feeling inadequate at age 40 for never having completed college, Joyce once again re-invented herself. This time she went back to school, graduating with honors with a music degree and winning a scholarship to Columbia University, which she declined because of her commitment to her children. "It annoyed my kids (who were in college and high school at the same time) that I was getting better marks than they were!" While at school, Joyce had read with relish about composition and theory—all the things that make musicians unique. A voracious reader, she now consumed all she could about comedy. She applied the knowledge and ideas to her comedy routines, always growing, always stretching herself to be better.

Joyce is an active participant in the success of her career. She got involved in theatre (wanting to be an actor but not prepared to leave her children) and anything that could help her open doors to expand her career. A film job got her in the doors of the Screen Actors Guild, where she used all the money she made on the film to pay her dues, and later the Actors Equity. She pushes and sells herself, belongs to many organizations and networks, is part of a speakers' association and a member of many talent agencies. "I pay a lot of dues!" Now opportunities find her. She does speaking engagements offering

"Laughercise" stress reduction and stress management workshops; she does stand-up comedy, emcees as a Corporate Jester, writes comedy, is a musician, singer and actor, and does corporate roasts. She recently did a movie, *The Boynton Beach Bereavement Club*, with actors Dyan Cannon and Joe Bologna. Her role was to improvise a scene in a furniture store when the man who was supposed to be her husband got sick. Suddenly she was told she was a widow…"You are a comedienne, improvise with some funny ideas." And she did. "Drama is easy," Joyce comments, "with comedy you have to think quickly."

Dubbed The Silver Fox of Comedy—"Grandma Does Stand-up," Joyce has appeared in major venues and organizations in New York, New Jersey, Connecticut and Florida. She has made several television and radio appearances, including "Saturday Night Live."

Joyce lives in Florida now (her grown children and grandchildren have followed her there) and jokes, "I hung up my snow shovel and called it a day. Be it ever so humble, there is no place like Florida, even with the hurricanes." She does the retirement community circuit, which she calls a "grown-up day camp" with their weekend Vegas-style shows. Not to remain dated, she has spread her wings to include comedy clubs for the 20- to 30-year-old set. Doubt crossed her mind (bringing back memories of when she first started in the business) as to whether she could write material that would relate to this young, hip and with-it crowd. Once again, she surprised herself and was a hit.

Joyce is under no pressure to retire. "My life is so exciting and I am having so much fun. I don't have to work 9 to 5. It is a commitment, but it is a choice that I make. I no longer need to work for money, so the pressure is off. I am not destined to sit in a park and feed pigeons. I would probably sit in the park and think of 50 ways to deal with pigeons…how to train 'em, sell 'em and cook 'em…" She chortles at the thought: "One day I am going to write a book about retirement…and pigeons."

Recently, at her high school reunion, after chatting up several of the women, Joyce realized that she was the only one to accomplish what she had said she would in her yearbook. She was an entertainer, she had raised her children and was a good wife. "The rest of the woman had lost themselves in marriage, devoted to their husbands and children."

Joyce's advice: "Family and children come first, but work around them. As they get older, you become freer, but don't let them hold you back. Find a way and pick something you enjoy. Fly with the wind!"

Joyce Kaye, Parkland, Florida. This contribution, ©2005-2006, is used with permission.

Shake out of the blues and give yourself permission to laugh. Contact Joyce Kaye Comedy Enterprises, 1-954-346-7418 fax 1-954-344-0629, 6190 NW 98th Drive, Parkland, Florida 33076, e-mail Joyce@JoyceKaye.com Web site www.joycekaye.com

• • •

"[A] group of senior citizens and I have put together another publishing company. All have visions of seeing their stories in print. I am also a senior. We are having the greatest time, helping each other and beginning a business. If anyone had told me when I was 40 that I would be working this much at age 69, and having soooo much fun, I'd have laughed in their face."

Edna Sniff, The Country Messenger Press, Okanogan, Washington,

e-mail edna@pctelecom.us

This contribution, ©2005-2006, is used with permission.

Chapter 16

Recovering From Cancer
Leila Peltosaari's Story

Cancer could delay but never derail Leila's dream to finish her self-published book *Illegally Easy™ Halloween Costumes for Kids*. Cancer further inspired her to write her greatest gift of all.

In the last days of summer when trees have burst their buds and are beginning to take on the vibrant hue of autumn, flowers are beginning to wilt and baby birds are taking flight, livin' should be easy, as the song says. But life does not always afford us simple pleasures. Fatal cells were multiplying and the big C reared its ugly head in Leila Peltosaari. "It's very serious," her doctor said, "you have breast cancer." The year was 2000. Leila, 53 years old, had separated from her husband three years before (they remain good friends). She had just moved to a new apartment with her daughter, Rina. "I was feeling good, and had begun work on the Halloween book."

Upon hearing the shocking news, Leila began to panic. Desperately wanting to complete her book, she left incoherent notes all over for her children, Rina and Albert, on what needed to be done to see her passionate project through to the end. "The book should survive even if I don't," Leila stated emphatically. Those words were the key to her survival.

Thinking of cancer was non-stop for Leila. The turning point happened when Albert surprised her with a Web site for her book. It gave her a boost of energy and a belief that there was a future after cancer.

Though suffering from "chemo brain" (forgetfulness) during the months of grueling chemotherapy treatments and weeks of radiation, Leila was determined to finish the book. "It was a positive focus to have something wonderful and exciting to do that was life-affirming." Talking about the book with her doctors was a distraction from her illness. "It gave me so much pleasure." The most exciting moment came during her radiation (following the chemo) when her husband and children arrived in the parking lot to hand her the final proofs. Leila was ecstatic. Touching those proofs, she knew she "was going to make it."

As a grand finale to her radiation, her books were printed. Jubilant, Leila wanted to celebrate, but with no energy, time or money to have an official book launch, she gave free copies to all those who took care of her in the hospital. She even included the parking lot attendant, who was thrilled to receive a copy. Each of the books were inscribed "Enjoy Life." Tears of joy streamed down the faces of the nurses, as they hugged Leila.

Recovery at home coincided with marketing and distributing the books. She submitted her book and won the Writer's Digest National Self-Published Book Award. An agent in Arizona saw the blurb written up about her, phoned her and thousands of orders poured in. As recently as this year, 2005, the *Better Homes and Gardens* Halloween special featured Leila's costume "Cinnamon Toast" from her book. As a result, she received orders for her book. *Illegally Easy*™ *Halloween Costumes for Kids* is still in print and can be obtained from Amazon.com.

On the surface, it seemed that Leila's book had been a financial success. But the truth was, she had poured three years of her heart into it and borrowed money to finance the costs of self-publishing. She was convinced that this would be her retirement money and that she would live happily ever after. "I was so sure that it would be a best-seller that I made a vow that if this book wasn't successful, I would not write another book." The reality was that market circumstances had changed, and people were no longer making their own costumes. Time-stressed lifestyles made it easier and less expensive to buy ready-made costumes. And not as many people owned sewing machines any longer. For Leila, that was a huge disappointment.

By 2003, Leila was 'antsy' for another project and in dire need of money to survive. She would either have to get a job or write another book. Despite her vow, she reasoned that just because one book did not work financially did not mean that another one would not work either. A book it was. That was her passion—Leila was a prolific writer. She had previously published a wide range of books.

Sitting at home alone one day, Sting's song *How Fragile We Are* was playing on the radio. Leila was still experiencing sadness and pain about her brush with death. Tears came to her eyes as she thought about a reoccurrence. Swaying to the music, she got up and instinctively danced. "I am dancing with fear," she thought. It was an "aha" moment. "I have to write a book about cancer to help women get through the experience. The title: *Dancing With Fear*. She was so excited at the prospect of this new book that her fear disappeared.

She was not qualified to write a medical book, and was not sure why anyone would want to hear just her story, but then it came to her. She would solicit other survivors to help her write the book, by amalgamating their fears, tips, hopes and dreams into the volume. It gave her energy and courage to continue with life. Stating a goal in public helps make it come true. "Ideas are very fragile. They need a little spark to get them burning," Leila says profoundly. Therefore, she told everyone she knew, including a friend in California, about the book of cancer tips she would write. Giving her friend an example, Leila informed her that during the course of her treatments, she had sewn a narrow bag with raw rice inside which she heated in the microwave and wrapped around her stomach to quell the cramps she had experienced after chemo. "It was better than any pills I was given."

That conversation had a domino effect. The friend worked for a language company that received calls requiring interpretations and translations. A breast cancer company representative called the line. The friend told the woman at the other end about Leila's ideas. That woman, also a breast cancer survivor, was so receptive to the book that she agreed to help Leila with suggestions and marketing. She even wrote a foreword for the book. "Her acceptance of my idea validated its importance. She was a high-profile woman, and she knew what she was doing."

In January 2004, Leila posted a notice in Dan Poynter's book publishing e-newsletter and on WebMD.com requesting stories from women around the world. The response was overwhelming: 125 women poured their hearts out. "It was heartwarming because I didn't know if anyone would respond," Leila recalls. Determined to include excerpts from all the submissions received, she worked furiously into the nights, reducing the manuscript from an unbelievable 2000 pages to 224. Leila considered it to be a "labor of love," noting "you don't count the hours when you can't wait to get up in the morning and get back to work." Her five-year journey since her cancer diagnosis had finally moved in a positive direction.

Most of the responses from others were positive. However, there were others she met along the way who felt the book would be too depressing for cancer patients and survivors to buy. One woman who had never experienced cancer thought the title should be "Dancing With Joy." Leila laughed, as only a cancer warrior would know the absurdity of such a notion. It just made her resolve stronger. "There are moments that you have to follow your dream. There will always be naysayers."

Just when you think you have life down pat, that things are going well, and that joy and success seem to be around the corner, life deals you another blow. Déjà vu. Mid-book, Leila began to experience physical symptoms that would not go away. A maddening itch invaded her body, and no doctors could find the cause. By January

2005, Leila found walking difficult and painful. Soon after, she could not drive. Leila was hospitalized in order to get all the tests done fast. An MRI scan indicated that she could have a massive cancer metastasis in her spinal cord, but a biopsy could cause permanent paralysis. It also revealed an aneurysm on her brain, which was inoperable because it was in a very dangerous spot. She would just have to live with that knowledge.

The doctors could not agree on a course of action about the spine growth, so a medical team formed. Leila rode an emotional roller coaster. She had no clue if she had cancer again, but neither did the medical team. Finally, the treatment agreed upon involved massive doses of steroids. If the tumor shrank, it would prove that it was just an inflammation. Once again, Leila fretted over the completion of her book, giving clear instructions to Rina to make sure her book was published. She felt it was imperative that she give to others a "hook of hope and a lifeline."

Thankfully, a later MRI confirmed that diagnosis of an inflammation. Nevertheless, Leila still could not walk. She had sudden and repeated severe shortness of breath. Knowing there was something wrong, her son called an ambulance to take her to Emergency. A CT Scan proved that she had a massive pulmonary embolism from a blood clot that had traveled to her lungs. The combination of Tamoxifen (a drug given to breast cancer patients if their tumors had been hormonally receptive) combined with the immobilization during the hospital stay just weeks earlier was deemed the cause. It seemed unlikely that Leila would survive the night, so the doctors insisted that she call her children. When she awoke the next day, surrounded by her loving family, she felt blessed to be alive.

There were just too many reasons for Leila to want life, including her devoted and loving children, the elation of the recent birth of her first grandchild—a girl, Philomène Arielle Joséphine—and, of course, her precious book *Dancing With Fear*. It is clear to Leila that the powers that be, agreed with her. "I feel that I deserve to be here and enjoy life. I am acutely aware of those special moments like a ray of sunshine on my face, my chosen solitude, or the company that I am with. It is the journey not the destination that matters, because who knows if we will ever get to where we thought we would."

Leila Peltosaari, 58, Verdun, Quebec.

This contribution, ©2005-2006, is used with permission.

For breast cancer warriors, *Dancing With Fear* will be their bible for advice, hope and inspiration and their connection to kindred spirits. For others, it will clarify the range of emotions that cancer survivors and patients endure. To order a copy of *Dancing With Fear*, contact Leila Peltosaari, Verdun, Quebec, Canada www.tikkabooks.com or leila@tikkabooks.com

Chapter 17

Overcoming Multiple Obstacles
Maureen Sherman's Story

Her arduous road to a productive life and sobriety was often marked with roadblocks and suicidal tendencies for Maureen Sherman. Her first suicide attempt came at the age of 15. After her first failure, Maureen says, "I tried to commit suicide on the installment plan—until I decided to go to any length to survive." She is a warrior. Her daunting roller-coaster ride through life has led her to thrive as a lifestyle coach and consultant, utilizing a variety of complementary approaches to proactive health.

Coming from a "multi-generational dysfunctional family," where her mother was deaf and her father was a violent, abusive alcoholic, just surviving had long been Maureen's focus. Her social skills were non-existent. At 18, she chose a man similarly wounded and mal-adapted as her father to be her husband. He lacked coping strategies and his defence mechanism was to be physically abusive. She endured four years and had a daughter (her only child) from the marriage. Her husband was eventually convicted of manslaughter and died five days later, after being given compassionate release due to illness following a lifetime in and out of jails. She lived with and then married another man. Her new husband was kind and gentle. Sadly, he could not cope with the tumultuous relationship and thought it easier to walk away 25 years ago.

For most of her adult life, Maureen remarks, "I always felt invisible, like a thing, not a person." Compounding the emotional turmoil, a serious car accident robbed her of her physical health. In spite of her inability to relate to others and her low self-esteem, Maureen was a hard worker and started her career as a ledger keeper for a bank. She made up for her lack of people skills by being "good at finding solutions." Detective work was her forte. Unfortunately, the car accident and her husband's departure had left her crushed. All too often, she began to rely on prescription drugs and alcohol for courage and strength.

When the bank downsized her to a teller, the stress overwhelmed her. Her recent diagnosis of having Attention Deficit Disorder (ADD) put into perspective the reason for her inability to stay on task when she was under extreme pressure. She resorted to more alcohol, prescription drugs, smoking and uncontrollable eating. For 10 years, she managed to function, but the bank jangled her around constantly, shifting her positions and providing her no support, until she hit rock bottom. Her brother, four years younger, and the only family member she had bonded with, killed his wife and then committed suicide. In a drunken stupor, she managed to call a suicide prevention line, which connected her to a recovery program. The bank refused to pay the $1000 fee. Maureen, desperate for a solution, chose to lose her house so that she could pay for the help she needed. After the fact, the bank relented and paid her back.

Maureen lived at a rehabilitation center for 28 days. "It was refreshing to deal with my problems [she had multiple health issues ranging from addiction to post-traumatic stress] and put myself first instead of being tormented and hiding." Upon her return to the bank, the stress of the job caused repeated physical problems, including many bouts of pneumonia. Compounding the problem was the bank's insensitivity. She was kept in a spiral of illness, fatigue, and then remission for three to six months each time over a three-year period. Her doctor recommended and reported to the bank that she take a leave of absence to regain her health and strength. After 13 years as an employee of the bank, living with stress and a tortured mind and body, her doctor told her frankly that if she continued working for the bank, she would die an early death. Upon her doctor's recommendation, she quit her job.

Now unemployed, Maureen had to sell her last material possession of any significance—her car. She went on employment insurance for a year. Traveling inward, she yearned to discover her life purpose and her identity as more than a mother, an employee, or someone with material things. "When everything was stripped away, at the core I was just a woman alcoholic."

Maureen volunteered for an environmental group. She also applied for disability insurance, which she is still on and trying to free herself from. "It is dehumanizing and self-defeating in many ways," she laments. She quit drinking and using prescription drugs. After eight years of being sober, she ended a 30-year smoking habit, trading that addiction for eating. She blew up to a hefty 248 pounds. Almost three years later, she addressed her food addiction and social issues. For many years, she worked with a gestalt therapist (the basis of the therapy is to weave the present with the past so you can see cause and effect, in a group setting). With the summers off, Maureen was able to "integrate what she learned during the year and try on new behaviors."

It was during one of those summers that Maureen examined her diet and health. She had so many health issues that when a doctor told her that she had better put her affairs in order because she would probably die soon, she went into survival mode. Venturing into a health food store seeking to change her diet, Maureen enquired about the possibility of volunteering. The women said no, but referred her to another store. That owner agreed.

Maureen tried one product, and shortly after, her debilitating migraines were gone. Her interest in regaining her health in natural ways was piqued. Maureen expressed interest in working in a health food store. Six months later, she got a call for a job that changed her life.

Maureen's father had recently died, leaving her $100,000. It was enough to put a substantial down payment on a house and buy a used car. Her naturopath, who was treating Maureen for free, moved her office to the health food store, and shortly thereafter, Maureen was offered a chance to work there on a part-time basis. A 72-year-old woman, who looked 55, came in to the store one day. The woman practiced reflexology. Maureen joked with her that she "did not think she could work with smelly feet all day long." The woman said she loved feet and that she had started her business when she was 65. She shared her knowledge of the business. The seed was planted that would become Maureen's passion.

Maureen was looking for a way to get off disability. Her fluctuating health and stamina meant that the only way for her to work was to have her own business. Although a bit skeptical at first, she took reflexology training and offered sessions for free to build up a client base, while continuing to work in the health food store. She looked for people who had circulatory and foot problems, and found herself on her way to an "awesome, empowering career." Soon her business grew and required more space. Initially, the naturopath allowed Maureen to use her office space on her days off. Eventually, as her clientele grew, Maureen's employer agreed to rent her office space. Maureen was also running the business from her home. At the five-year point in her business, some of the negative conditions that had affected her life years before were beginning to resurface. She reverted to some of her old thinking—that she could never be a success, that she was unlovable and that her clients would "jump ship" (they never did). Through a series of events, she was forced to downsize and make her home the official office.

Loving reflexology and the detective work involved in helping people deal with chronic illness, Maureen's past experience gave her the keen ability to hone in on people's problems. Soon she was coaching them to higher levels of health and vitality, focusing on body mind and spirit wholeness, utilizing various training experiences and protocols. Slowly she moved into a new and comfortable realm. Her clients were experiencing successes in various areas. She achieved results, yet she was still not 100 percent convinced that she could take clients where she herself had not been able to go. She knew she had to overcome the "conditioning" of years past.

Two years ago, when Maureen was about to give up the career she loved, a conference in Florida changed everything. She overheard a participant talk about a "bio resonance" session that had made a difference in her way of being. Again skeptical, Maureen began to explore the technology. After training sessions and thorough examination, Maureen experienced rapid results. Convinced that the technology was worthwhile, she purchased a machine.

Maureen is now firmly back on track. Her successful methodology as a Certified WaveMaker™ Coach, using a whole-person approach to the mind and body, is not New Age, says, Maureen, but "just common sense and down to earth." Maureen's clients attest to the results. A lifelong learner, Maureen is always investigating and "incorporating complementary, non-invasive techniques, assisting others living with chronic illness and life conditioning that limits their hope and enjoyment of life." Always evolving and reworking, Maureen plans to phase out reflexology, nutritional and glyconutrient perspectives over the next two years to concentrate on coaching for personal and career development using Bio Resonance/EFT.

Success to Maureen means supportive healthy relationships, personal power to control her own destiny, and freedom from past conditioning. Being financially independent remains a keen desire. Her belief is strong that her dream is waiting just around the bend. One of her loyal clients testifies that Maureen's "devotion, her sincerity, her compassion and her knowledge are assets that will resonate in all her endeavors." There is no doubt that Maureen's courage and inspiration will be rewarded by success.

Maureen Sherman, 59, St. Catharines, Ontario.

This contribution, ©2005-2006, is used with permission.

To experience quality of life and optimum health naturally, contact: Maureen Sherman, "Soulworks Certified Wholistic Lifestyle Coach and Consultant" 905-685-7235, e-mail Maureen@mergetel.com

The best is yet to be; intention is the key.

Chapter 18

It Pays to Volunteer
Lisa Coulson's Story

Lisa Coulson does not have a lot of material things, but her life, she says, "is rich in cats." These days, she happily shares her apartment with two sister cats retrieved from a cat-rescue organization. Fifteen years ago, Lisa Coulson was miserable.

Running a corporate library for a manufacturer and managing a corporate communications program for the engineering office and factory staff was good until the company started to downsize. By the fourth round, Lisa found herself out of a job. The company had installed computers two years prior to Lisa's layoff and she had wanted to learn all about them. The company provided training for the engineers only, so Lisa lost out.

However, the skills she acquired in that job worked their magic, and she landed another position, again in manufacturing and working with engineers. It was only a contract job. Computers once again factored into her employment situation. The manufacturing company had arranged with a local college to provide training for its factory workers, and Lisa provided administrative support to the department delivering the training. She was able to learn bits and pieces, but not enough to make her adept. When the training department contract expired, she moved to another administrative position at the college; however, that department was in a state of reorganization and things were moving too fast for Lisa to keep up. "I felt off balance," she recalls sadly. For the third time in a short period, Lisa found herself unemployed.

Shipping out one resume after another in 1998, it soon became apparent to her that her possibilities for employment were directly proportional to her computer skills. She was not in the financial position to take a proper course, so she took a computer course run by Human Resources Development Canada (now Human Resources Skills Development Canada, HRSDC) that was free. Lisa facetiously calls it a "quick and dirty" program, because it ran for three months and included six or seven software programs, as well as many related topics. "I got a sense of how things worked, but not how to apply the knowledge. Although everyone in the class gained a little knowledge about computers, there was just not enough time to learn everything."

Lisa made a vital decision. Without proper computer training, she was not going to get a job. There was only one way that she could afford to do something about it: she owned a small townhouse and even though she had a lot of debt, she did have some equity in the property. Her younger son was ready to make his own life, so the timing was good. Selling the house left her with enough funds to rent a small apartment and attend a private college for a one-year course in digital design. The rub was that the school was in Toronto and she lived in Burlington, over an hour away. It cost twenty dollars a day for transportation to downtown Toronto. Five times, she tried to apply for a student loan, only to be rejected each time. Her questions got her nowhere. There were no other people willing to support her.

"Freaking out about the transportation costs, I started packing a small bag on a Monday, going to the college, and sleeping on the floor in the computer lab until Friday." Into the last semester, Lisa could not carry on with her desired endeavors. Exhausted, feeling demoralized and with no money to pay rent, she "offloaded" her apartment to a friend, contents included. She had her older son take some of her treasured children's mementoes, and she gathered up a suitcase with her necessities. She headed to Toronto, called a women's shelter, and moved in.

The beauty of serendipity is that it sometimes comes to us when we are in despair. At the same time that Lisa moved to the shelter, another woman arrived as well. Originally from Toronto, Susan had been injured on the job and was on Workmen's Compensation for perpetuity. She had been overseas, and had come back to tie up loose ends. An arrangement to stay with a friend didn't work out, and Susan too had to live at the shelter. Her plan was to start a business. Susan had heard about MicroSkills, with its unique women's programs, which included Self-Employment Training for Women. She asked Lisa if she wanted to go with her. Lisa, not familiar with the city and anxious to learn, happily agreed.

While there, a flyer caught Lisa's attention. It was for a free (if you were receiving social assistance benefits, which she was) Web designer program. Perfect, thought Lisa. Examining the year-long program convinced her that it would be as good as the one she had been taking at the private college. Lisa yearned to complete the original digital design program so she could get a good job, but lack of transportation money was still a problem. Time had also become an issue: when she arrived in Toronto, Lisa had two more months before her pass card to the private college would expire. Unfortunately, she was stuck in the west end of the city and the college was downtown. Social Services provided 25 dollars a month for everything the shelter didn't supply —and that meant Lisa had to pay any bus fares herself. She had to use that money to look for a permanent residence and purchase any incidental necessities, leaving little to nothing left to chase a dream. Eventually, the pass card expired, and with it any opportunity of completing the original program.

Back at the shelter, Lisa was being asked about what direction she wanted to go in her life. Lisa showed them the flyer, telling them, "If I can pick up the smarts to learn the computer efficiently, than my long-term goal is to get back into corporate communications." It was a good plan. Lisa went to an interview, fit the criteria of being a low-income earner and showed them that she was gung-ho to get on with it. "I was appreciative of the opportunity, especially because it included transportation support to those in need. MicroSkills programs for women are designed to include support services that address the many barriers encountered by low-income, immigrant and racial-minority women."

By September of that year, Lisa was proudly occupying her seat at MicroSkills, anxious to get on with her life and finish what she so deeply desired. She never saw Susan again, but the impact of their meeting was fortunate. The 20 women in her class were a mixed bag of experience. Many of them had never used a computer. Lisa had the advantage of having most of the basics. Instead of wasting her time doing nothing while they were learning Microsoft Office, she began to help the others. "It was fun," Lisa remembers fondly. Unbeknownst to her, it was the beginning of her new career. She knew some Adobe software, and helped the women with Photoshop. She was learning too (assisting others is one of the best ways to understand something, according to psychologists), but she did not know how to troubleshoot problems and fix them, especially while at home. A course called Network Administration beckoned her. She envisioned getting her Microsoft Certified Professional (MCP) designation.

Lisa reminisces affectionately about her instructor for that course: "All the instructors I had in my previous courses, wherever I took them, were good, but Vera was the best technical instructor I had ever run across. She was always compassionate, patient, extremely knowledgeable, and very good at explaining the various topics clearly. Vera was certainly a national treasure." Nevertheless, several months into that course, Lisa was becoming seriously overwhelmed. Ten- to

12-hour days, doing schoolwork seven days a week, was taking its toll. Luckily for Lisa, by this time she had found an apartment close to MicroSkills that was affordable on social assistance. Still, she was unable to complete any of the exams. "I was burned out, just spinning my wheels." To relieve the pressure, she relinquished her academics and started volunteering at MicroSkills. One opportunity was teaching for the next Web-design class. There were no more exams to study for, no more assignments to prepare, just prep work for each class. Most of the women did well in her course—an achievement that bode well for her future. Next, she immersed herself in a new project: setting up and cataloging hundreds of books, using software especially designed for resource libraries. Lisa was not consciously considering her future at that moment, she was just trying to get her life back in focus.

Several months later, when she had completed her work on the library collection, Lisa was surprised and thrilled to be offered a part-time job at MicroSkills. After five months, the job became permanent. That was four years ago. Lisa now works in the Employment Resource Center helping people job search and prepare their resumes and cover letters. She also prepares workshops, creates flyers on the computer, and even troubleshoots computer problems for clients! Some of her work involves editing and research, which she really enjoys. "There are lots of opportunities to get into all kinds of things," Lisa says, happy with her employer and hard-won stability.

Lisa's "blood, sweat and tears" while she upgraded her computer skills, enhanced by her gracious act of volunteering, have paid off. "I had been doing all that work for years to get employed! Now she needs only to go home at the end of each day and enjoy her cat companions.

• • •

It was more than Lisa's computer skills that made her noticeable at MicroSkills: it was her ability to avail herself wholeheartedly to the needs of the center and the clients who occupied it. Lisa wishes to impart her wisdom on the subject of **volunteering**:

1.   Take a volunteer opportunity seriously, as if it was the only job you are likely to get. Put all you've got into it.

2.   Volunteering can open doors. You can choose doors number one, two or three. Whichever one you choose, make the most out of it.

3.   Volunteering is not just about why the work is useful to you. It is more about how you can make a difference in the organization.

4.   Volunteer work is as valid as a paid position because the situation you're in and skills you use or learn are the same. The only difference is the pay aspect.

5.   Volunteering is an opportunity to show what you can do. If someone waves an opportunity at you, grab it. It is a real-time advertisement of who you are and what you can do.

Lisa Coulson, Toronto, Ontario.

This contribution, ©2005-2006, is used with permission.

Lisa Coulson, Information Officer, Community MicroSkills Development Centre Toronto, ON Canada 416-247-7181 x201 (Employment Resource Centre) fax 416-247-1877 www.microskills.ca

Chapter 19

Love Your Community
Daniela Sher's Story

The immigrant experience is usually daunting. Language barriers, job searching with no experience in the land you have come to, sometimes no family or friends to provide emotional support—all this and more can leave the immigrant in a perpetual state of disarray. It would be easy to give up and just settle for mediocrity. Daniela (Danguole by birth) Sher was not going to let that happen. She has started a life in a new world not once, but twice. She has a dream and it is within reach.

Daniela hails from Lithuania—a country where, in the 1970s, anti-Soviet sentiment was high. Underground youth movements were making noise about independence. The Shers wanted freedom for their children and a better future. Daniela and her husband, who is Jewish, made the decision to live in Israel where his parents were. The Soviet Union had no diplomatic relationship with Israel, but because her husband was Jewish, they were given the restricted but legal opportunity to emigrate. "Fearing we would never see the rest of our family again—emigrants were not permitted to return to Lithuania—all our relatives came to bid their tearful goodbyes," she recalls of the heart-rending time.

The Shers arrived in the "land of milk and honey" with good educations, two small children and four pieces of luggage: one filled with pictures, one with diapers for their infant daughter, one with clothes for their son, and the fourth with a few bits of clothing and necessities for themselves. Each 'head' leaving the Soviet Union was allowed the meager sum of one hundred dollars.

They had mixed feelings about their new home. The country was beautiful, with lush fertile farmlands and forests, vast deserts and dramatic cliffs. The children were happy and attended a good school. Although Daniela had a master's degree in Linguistics, majoring in German Language and Literature, she gratefully attended a teacher's seminar for immigrants in bookkeeping and administration, paid for by the Israeli Government. Even though she was a teacher in Lithuania, she did not have the requirements to be a teacher in Israel. The one-and-a-half-year bookkeeping course they provided gave her the necessary license to teach high school in Israel. She never went to work as a teacher. She was fortunate to land a good job with benefits at a bank as a bookkeeper/adminis-trator. Her husband had a job with IBM. He also had the dangerous task of clearing mines for the Israeli army.

A year turned into over 10. Her husband's older brother was killed in a car accident and his dad was ill with cancer. Family obligations kept them grounded. Finally, the heat that gave her migraines, the uncertainty of the political stability of the country and family pres-sures made them pack their bags and move to Canada.

Prior to leaving for Canada, in 1988, Daniela was fortunate that her husband arranged by special visa for her and her daughter to travel to Lithuania to see Daniela's mother. Trying to change the image and structure of his beleaguered nation, President Mikhail Gorbachev of the Soviet Union relaxed the return of émigrés to their homeland. It was an intense emotional encounter between the three generations. They had been separated for 11 years.

Canada offered them financial security for her husband. When he obtained his working papers and landed immigrant status for Canada, he quit his position in Israel and went to Canada to see if he could get a job at IBM there before his family moved. Four interviews later, a job was offered to him. He went back to Israel to discuss it with Daniela and they decided he should take the job in Ontario. On his final pre-settlement trip to Ontario, he rented a house and went back to Israel to help his family move. They arrived in a new land, knowing only one person, to an empty house where they had to sleep on the floor. At least this time they came with some money that they had saved from a decade of working in Israel.

There was little opportunity for Daniela, however. She did not speak English and her youngest son was a toddler. She had no babysitter and preferred to stay home with him. Although offered the benefit of taking English classes, she instead chose to be self-taught. "Reading, reading, reading—books and newspapers. I was good with languages. Learning English was a great achievement."

By January 1990, Daniela realized that her husband's income was not enough to cover their household responsibilities. Without a clue as to how to search for a job in Canada, but because she had professional credentials (albeit foreign) in bookkeeping and administration, she began to explore the possibilities. Her English was now passable. She took a quick course at a college to learn English terms for her profession.

Scouring the ads of a local Lithuanian newspaper, she saw a job posting for a bookkeeper. The terms she had learned in the college class proved useful and she got the job. For eight years, she did her due diligence there, but when the Board of Directors needed to reduce their administrative expenses, her position was eliminated. They offered her a part-time contract in bookkeeping. She agreed and was able to work from home. She found herself bored at home, though.

While still in the office, she had noticed that when she was around people and activity, she thrived. Deciding that she was a social person, she quit her dead-end job. The whole time Daniela was working, she had immersed herself in the Lithuanian cultural community as a volunteer. That was an activity that she did not stop when she quit her job. Not only did she love what she was doing, she wanted to keep herself "busy and productive"…in the sector she felt most passionate about. She still maintains a stronghold in the Lithuanian Canadian Foundation as Executive Committee secretary, and as treasurer of the Women's Auxiliary Group.

Daniela speaks proudly of being the lead person in concert organizing, fundraising, promoting and writing articles for famous mezzo-soprano Judita Leitaite, soloist from the National Philharmonic Society of Lithuania. There were many other prestigious, successful concerts organized by Daniela for other performers, as well. The more she got involved in cultural events and experienced the sheer joy her volunteer work gave her, the closer she was to formulating her dream. "I would like to be the volunteer co-coordinator for the Canadian Opera House or the National Ballet," she states affirmatively.

By the spring of 2004, Daniela was determined to work again, her exact career aspirations gelling but not yet firm. In the process of seeking employment, she decided to take advantage of some government-funded programs to help ease her transition. All the volunteer work we do does not translate often enough into confidence when applying for a paid position. Daniela was no exception. She wanted to make sure she would be oozing confidence when she applied for jobs. "I needed help to focus on my goals."

The first course called Breakthrough—an enhanced job search program—provided her with the tools she needed to prepare her resume and cover letter, learn how to act in interviews, how to make a "cold call" and how to network. It also gave her the opportunity to brush up on her computer skills.

After the month-long course, she took a career and employability course for women called Focus. After a myriad of assessments, Daniela emphatically knew that she "did not want to be a bookkeeper." However, she wanted to work with people. "I nailed the areas of employment and careers that can fit my passion, education, skills and knowledge. The sectors of my interests were: not-for-profit and retail." She examined ads in those areas, noting the skills necessary for the positions and made efforts to upgrade in those areas.

In August 2004, Daniela utilized the results and skills she had acquired and sought employment in her preferred fields. Never close-minded, she saw every experience as an opportunity to learn new things. Networking with a woman in a store about the possibility of a job, lead her to another store—a women's clothing boutique where the owner was looking for a manager. "I was lucky because they were looking for somebody to hire. I can say that I was hired on the spot. My goal for this job was to experience a sector in which I hadn't previously worked. It was good experience for me dealing with people. I really enjoyed that job. During the interview, I was calm and confident."

December came with a new opportunity. A good reputation percolates through communities, garnering attention. Daniela's character preceded her and she was known in her community. She was offered a part-time job as a volunteer-coordinator at a nursing home. Using the skills she had acquired from the government-sponsored courses, she prepared for the interview. With confidence and poise, she says, "I did not feel any fear. I was in control of my emotions. I was hired even without the certificate (Volunteer Management Certificate)."

Daniela recognized the importance of obtaining that credential and she pursued it. She is proud to have graduated from this course and plans to continue her upgrading for certification in fundraising. She states with confidence, "I am following my heart. I now work in the area in which I planned to work. I'm enjoying my work very much and I'm doing well.

Daniela's future plans? "To secure employment in the theater as a volunteer co-coordinator." The theatre experience will only become richer for all, on the day that Daniela takes on that role!

Danguole-Daniela Sher, 54, Thornhill, Ontario.

This contribution, ©2005-2006, is used with permission.

The possibilities for volunteering are endless. The benefits are priceless. Unless your reason for being out of the workplace is health-related, taking the opportunity to volunteer is an important step for many reasons:

- Employers increasingly recognize that the experience and responsibility that go along with volunteering is equal to that of paid employment.
- Volunteering allows you to explore areas of interest to see if you like a particular industry.
- It gives you a concrete purpose to fill in spare time, closing gaps in your resume.
- It gives you something productive to do if finding employment is not happening immediately and you are feeling frustrated.
- It gives you an answer to the question "What do you do?" if you are uncomfortable with stating that you are unemployed.
- It keeps you up-to-date with current trends in a particular industry.
- It offers you opportunities to learn new or improved skills. These can be hard or soft skills. *See List of Terms You Should Know for Job Searching.*
- It may allow your creativity and resourcefulness to shine.
- You may discover interesting careers or new jobs within the same career.
- It gives you the opportunity to network with others, make connections, open new doors and build relationships. *See Chapter 5, Networking, Networking, Networking.*
- For immigrants, volunteering provides all-important Canadian experience. It is an efficient and effective way to speed up your job search process.
- It can turn into paid employment.
- It raises your self-esteem, knowing that you are doing something valuable.
- It helps other people and allows you to give back to society.

Volunteering is a commitment—the same as a paid position. Pick a place where you will derive the most benefit for future job possibilities. You may get lucky and just be able to walk into a volunteer position, but probably you will have to apply and go through an interview process as if it were a paying job. This is especially true if you are working in a social-service setting, dealing with children or vulnerable people who require protection under the law. You may be asked to pay for and submit to a police check. Do your homework about the organization just as if you were researching a company where you are seeking employment. If you like what you are doing and the people you are working with, you will put more effort into your volunteer job.

So where do you start? Sometimes you need not look any further than your immediate community. Schools, hospitals, community centers, local cultural centers and religious institutions all provide many opportunities to strut your stuff. Local community volunteer centers should be listed in your telephone directory under Community Services—Volunteer. *See Resources section.*

If you are interested in the non-profit industry and wish to pursue a career in it, check your preferred college or university to see if they offer credit/diploma courses. It is a growing sector.

Chapter 20

And She Wrote It in English:
An Immigrant's Experience
Grace Tallar's Story

English was Grace Tallar's third language. Therefore, the probability of writing a self-help book in English was slim. Nevertheless, a gutsy, knowledgeable, determined Grace Tallar took a great leap of faith and landed on her feet.

An immigrant from Poland, Grace came to Canada over 20 years ago, as the black cloud of Marshall Law loomed over her country. Grace was a single mother, and life in Poland was not conducive to raising a young child or finding a suitable job.

Since her arrival in Canada, Grace has termed herself "a frequent newcomer," moving from coast to coast 13 times in the past 10 years. Along with each move came the fear of starting all over again. "My fear was survival. We lived off credit cards. We were always in debt. I clearly remember all of the emotions and difficulties involved in the long process of rebuilding my personal and professional life in a new country. Regardless of your skills, each time you make a change, your self-esteem goes down and you lose concentration. There is an urgency to find a job, but fear of weakness will prevent you from moving forward. I was seriously depressed. I lost my confidence. I lost my main identity."

However, Grace has learned that life's labors can open new doors if you are willing to open your mind, and she adds new meaning to the phrase "been there, done that." "I don't think there are many jobs that I haven't done," she jokes. She has been a laborer, a manager (in the aerospace industry as the first woman manager, she developed and improved management systems in North America and Europe), a trainer, a marketer, a saleswomen, a real estate agent, a writer and an entrepreneur.

She is a lifelong learner, with a journalism degree from Warsaw University, Business and Administration degree from McGill University, and her Real Estate and Sub-Mortgage Broker degree from the University of British Columbia. Interestingly, however, the area Grace has had the most experience in is job searching, having been "out there, pounding the pavement for years." She wanted to utilize her own experiences and knowledge to help others, especially immigrants because "they face much deeper emotional barriers—language and social—than any other group."

"My dream, since the 1970s was to be a writer," says Grace. Sometimes dreams are slow in the making, so that when they come true, they are all the more powerful. In 1985, Grace, who had remarried in Montreal, gathered up the necessary writing tools and her dog and temporarily left her family with the instructions that she was not to be bothered. She headed for the family cottage in the Eastern Townships of Quebec. After days of being isolated, she only managed to cobble together a few paragraphs. "Some writer," she chided herself. It would take 11 years before her dream became a reality—a book, co-written in Polish with a colleague from Montreal.

The job market was changing. Separatism in Quebec was a growing concern, and Grace moved into a new career, in a different company, in a different province. Now in Vancouver, Grace got a contract with BC-based Intrawest. They were starting projects in Poland and needed a Polish-speaking person with project management and real estate skills. She was sent to Poland seeking new business opportunities for the firm. Little did she know she would also find her dream waiting around the corner.

A keen observer of human nature, Grace noticed people's general difficulties in finding a job. Grace and her colleague wanted to share what they had learned in Canada. The book *50 Career Ideas: First Step to Financial and Professional Independence* was born.

Grace became enamored with the subject of the job search. On a quest for self-discovery because of the emotions she had experienced about her own job searches, a fortuitous newspaper advertisement about a course on 'Emotional Intelligence' caught her eye. She enrolled in the course. Becoming adept on the issue, she became a trainer, creating her own program. For seven years, over 5000 people trained under Grace. Poland was a huge market with loads of money just waiting to be exploited. There was a book waiting in the wings.

Fear, that ever present bubble that envelopes most of us, struck Grace once again. "I was not a Ph.D. in a field that is scientific. I had no idea if anyone would publish my book." But publish she did. Her first book had been published by a Canadian publisher in Poland. Her second and third books, *ABC of Emotional Intelligence* (based on her training program) and *How to Find a Job in 30 Days*, were published by the most renowned Polish publisher Studio-Emka.

Grace spent her time traveling between Poland and Canada. Her dream of writing a book had come to fruition, but to write in English was her next ambition. In order to do that, she knew she had to improve her English.

Returning to Ontario from a stint in Vancouver, Grace wanted to put down roots—she and her husband were now grandparents and Grace wanted to be close to her daughter and grandson. She needed a survival job so that they could afford the home she and her husband had bought. Grace was not a nine-to-fiver. After years of being a career woman, traveling the world and having interesting, exotic and high-profile jobs, she desired something else to nurture her soul. "It was not my personality to be tamed into that routine. I wanted to get back to my family."

She volunteered at the YMCA, helping trainers for a youth employment services program. On her third day back in Ontario, while driving to the grocery store, she passed an Employment Resource Centre. Knowing that finding employment was her area of expertise, she put in a resume for a position as a career counselor for a government-sponsored program to help immigrants get jobs. They were impressed with her new ideas. Within two weeks, she got the job. While there, she noticed gaps in the training programs and became disillusioned that the people she was trying to help get jobs were not responsive to suggestions. She knew she could help these people by writing a book for them on Emotional Intelligence, but building up personal financial stability had became a priority—she couldn't simply take the time off to write.

By the summer of 2004, Grace felt confident enough in her language ability and her idea to take the plunge of being a full-time writer. She bankrolled herself to have the funds to self-publish, set up her Web site, and pay all the expenses that would come with the project. She worked steadily to get the book written and produced in print, merging her many learned skills in the process. The result is a well-written, thoroughly researched, provocative and informative book, *Get Hired on Demand—An Advanced Career Guide—for Internationally Trained Professionals*, written in English.

Writing and producing a book is one thing, marketing is another. Grace is now on a whirlwind marketing frenzy, leaving little time to relax. Slowly but surely, her grandiose endeavor is being rewarded. She is recognized as a speaker extraordinaire, even though she has a great fear of speaking. She has caught the attention of the media. Her Web site action has increased a hundredfold. Her marketing ideas flow like a winding river as she reaches deep within herself, finding fulfillment, bursting with self-confidence that all her labor will have a happy ending.

Grace is well aware that achievement involves many sacrifices—personal, family and financial. She is still striving for financial security, but knows that her dogged determination and positive attitude will get her to that place. Every experience brings her one step closer to her goal. She believes that if people do not take risks, the greater threat is emotional stagnation and loss of self-esteem. That is not a role model for anyone. Grace offers this stellar advice: "We have only one chance on earth. There are ups and downs and the successful person has to stand up one more time than she falls. Never give up any of your dreams. Be patient and persist."

Grace Tallar, 54, Aurora, Ontario.

This contribution, ©2005-2006, is used with permission.

To obtain a copy of *Get Hired on Demand*, for on-line career training and subscription to her newsletter, or to hire Grace as a speaker, contact Grace Tallar at 905-726-8005 or info@newcomersupplies.com Web site www.NewcomerSupplies.com .

Chapter 21

Filling That Niche
Marnie Scott's Story

Observing the needs of pregnant women who were in the penal system, Marnie Scott was determined to help women get through this emotional time in their lives, especially if their pregnancy was not planned.

Marnie began her career as a graduate with a Correctional Worker diploma and post-graduate studies in the same field. Counseling was part of her background, training she utilized as a correctional officer. For five years she worked with young offenders and adults at a local jail, but was only able to get a full-time contract position. She had no benefits and felt abused by the system. When the jail closed, she was offered a transfer, which she declined, even though her wages were good. Having miscarried once before while on the job, she desperately wanted a child. When she became pregnant again, she knew that the unpredictable 12-hour shifts and stress in the workplace would be unacceptable. Thus, her daughter, Emma, was the impetus to propel her career.

Her pregnancy followed by the first year of Emma's life meant that Marnie had been away from the workplace for two years, except for a short stint as a part-time waitress. She looked after her daughter and at night took some classes. She also volunteered with Children's Aid. She spent her time "evaluating" her goals and determining what direction she wanted to go now that she was a mother.

"I felt very overwhelmed and discouraged by the fact that I had really struggled to get through college to become a correctional officer and now that career no longer seemed like an option. While I was thrilled to become a mother, I felt as though I was giving up a part of myself. I was back at square one, trying to figure out what to do with my life and I hadn't even finished paying off the student loans for my first career yet! I applied for many jobs, but what I really wanted was a career."

A seed had been planted years before, and Marnie had been slowly working on the steps unaware that it would come to fruition. Her dream was to open a baby boutique and pregnancy help center. Her family was supportive, but many others were critical of her leaving a "government position." Marnie was determined to forge ahead anyway, but she knew she needed guidance.

While applying for maternity leave, she had picked up a brochure about a self-employment program, sponsored by Human Resources and Skills Development Canada (HRSDC). Encouraged, she followed it up. The road that is paved with good intentions does not always take you where you want to go in a hurry and so it is with government programs. Marnie found roadblocks everywhere she turned. Challenged but determined, she was motivated to see the process through to the end. She made endless phone calls trying to obtain information.

Finally, after many weeks, she was able to access the qualifications of the program and she applied in writing. Being on maternity leave, collecting Employment Insurance (EI) and having a viable business concept made her eligible. She presented her idea to a panel who thought it would work. There was no fee for the program at that time.

Thereafter, for seven intensive weeks, Marnie attended class. The program included everything from developing a business plan to networking, marketing and branding. It even included access to a personal coach for 48 weeks after starting the business. "It was a phenomenal way to get practical business experience," Marnie gushes about the program she just completed.

Marnie is now the proud occupant of a leased store in a new building, a block away from her home. Her baby boutique offers a unique line of products, including baby clothing designed by Marnie and sewn by other women. Half of the retail space is filled with gently used baby furniture, clothes and baby gift baskets, all purchased by Marnie on a consignment basis, that parents can buy inexpensively. Working with her assistant in the free counseling help center, Marnie will listen and give the women non-medical advice and options. Because she lives in a small town, access to pregnancy health services is limited. She hopes that a year from now she can connect with the Regional Municipality to have a full-fledged Pregnancy Health Center. Her mother, who lives behind her, is willing and able to babysit her granddaughter, Emma.

Marnie has fulfilled her dream of opening her baby boutique and pregnancy health center. Her new work environment is, in her words, "conducive to family and personally rewarding." It will utilize her college education, provide a service to others and add income to her household, something that makes her particularly proud.

Marnie Scott, Port Perry, Ontario.

This contribution, ©2005-2006, is used with permission.

If you wish to purchase a unique baby gift, rent a new-arrival sign, use the memorable baby shower planning service, make an "upscale resale" contribution, or if you require pregnancy counseling, please contact Marnie Scott, **The Cuddle Bunny Co.** at 1-905-985-9956/ toll-free 1-866-736-BABY (2229), 158 Water St. Unit 101, Port Perry, Ontario, Canada L9L 1C4.

Tips for the Self-Employed

I did not specifically go looking for only self-employed women when I requested stories for this book. Most of the women who responded had found that self-employment was the best route for them to take. Self-employment could be the answer to your dreams also. Depending on the nature of your business, self-employment can provide some or all of the following benefits:

- the empowerment of being in control—you are the boss, you make the decisions;
- raised self-esteem—you are doing something you feel is valuable;
- the opportunity to follow a passion;
- flexibility of hours;
- the convenience of working from home;
- the reward of filling a niche in the marketplace.

The Rewards Can Be Delicious!

"Joining Mary Kay has been extremely positive for me. I have received excellent training at a professional level and this has raised my self-esteem, restored my confidence and completely transformed my whole outlook."

Farida Khan, 54, Markham, Ontario.

This contribution, ©2005-2006, is used with permission.

Owning your own business can be a risky venture. The statistics vary on the failure rates of business, but whether it is 50 percent or 95 percent within the first few years, that rate is high. Serious considerations have to be made before you decide to go this route.

There are so many valuable Web sites and books available to help you successfully run a business (this book could have been written on the subject of self-employment alone) that my aim in this section is to prompt questions about things to consider before plunging into deep waters without a life jacket.

Questions to Ponder

What do you want to do? (a particular service or product)
See Chapter 3: Things to Consider Pre-employment—Go through the exercise of self-assessment. You can also pay trained professionals in order to be assessed.

Do you want to be a local or international business?

Will you be starting a new business or buying an established one?
If buying an established business, it should be assessed to see if it is financially viable.

Do you have the financial resources to back your idea?
- How much will it cost to start up? Don't forget to consider the following:
  - Insurance
  - Office rental/purchase
  - Lawyer, accountant/bookkeeper or other professional fees
  - Renovations
  - Equipment
  - Supplies
- How much money will you need for the near future?
  - If you go to a financial institution, do you have a business plan? (Each bank may have a business plan format).

Who will do the bookkeeping?

Are there people you can go to for help?

Do you have the support of your life partner?

Do you want to work from home?

Will your line of work be profit or non-profit?

Are you interested in a franchise?

Is it feasible for you to work from home? Do you have the space?

Can you balance family and business—will you be able to end your workday?

Will there be distractions—children, pets, chores, social calls, ready access to snacks—and do you have the discipline to stay focused?

Do you want a business partner?

Will you have employees?

What will you name your company?

Should you incorporate your business?

Where will you get your supplies?

What will your hours be?

How will you market yourself?
> *Hint: If a 'Pet Rock' can get market attention, anyone, with the right promotional techniques and vision, can be successful!*

Chapter 22

Thinking Out of the Box
Karen Hatcher's Story

The client is shocked when he opens the door to find standing there a petite, blond woman with a "Cheshire cat" grin announcing that she is the electrician he called. He jokingly asks her if she needs a ladder to get on the ladder. She smiles. The man is skeptical that a woman can do what she claims. but he's not sure how to delicately deal with the situation, so she is allowed in to do her job.

Once Karen Hatcher (nicknamed Smiley and Sparky) does her job, the man is duly impressed. Karen, whose bubbly personality oozes enthusiasm with every breath she takes, has set very high standards for herself. Her mission always is to "provide the very best customer service that I can. All my customers are wonderful people. They always thank me and say I make them feel right at ease from the start. I train my helpers to think and act the same way too." Karen's motto: "Always show respect toward others and be compassionate to all of their feelings."

So how does one go from working at a factory job for 15 years to becoming an electrician? The answer is that it takes a lot of soul searching, a stringent commitment to see the training through, sacrifice and money (Karen did not have much of the latter).

In November of 2002, Karen, a single mom of two children, was laid off from what was admittedly a dead-end job in a cookie factory. She yearned to go to university to become a teacher, but the costs were prohibitive. Depressed and rejected that she could not support her children and was not able to follow her dreams, Karen applied for other factory jobs. On too many occasions, she was told that she was over-qualified. Suggestions were made that she consider the skilled trades. Self-assessment tests reconfirmed that Karen had the potential to be a master electrician. "Why not?" she thought, given that her father was an electrician and her brothers were skilled tradesmen.

When applying for Employment Insurance, she had to attend a day information session where she filled out a job-history form. She was told of a retraining and upgrading program sponsored by what was then Human Resources Development Canada, now know as Human Resources and Skills Development (HRSDC). The forms were endless. HRSDC only accepts people who are upgrading in a similar field, not for a career change. Because Karen had 15 years of factory work behind her and high mechanical and spatial skills, she was one of the few accepted into an electrical and network cabling pre-apprentice course after many tests and more forms to get licensing. She was offered 100 percent funding for the apprenticeship program.

In the four months it took for Karen to find out if she was accepted, she prepared to go back to school, which she had been away from for 16 years, by taking a math course. Although she was exempt from the normal process for apprenticeship, she "still had to write the grueling exams to prove her knowledge and skills." The only female among 16 males, Karen soon become "one of the boys." They all supported one another.

Karen had already shown her talent for things electrical, a genetic trait she picked up early in her life from her father, by taking toasters apart and putting them back together (much to the chagrin of her mother). Going back to school for theory, cramming for exams, keeping up with homework, and being a single mom, however, was a daunting task. Her family and friends rallied around her to keep her buoyed. "My kids are my inspiration to be the best that I can be," says Karen. "I want them to see how rewarding it is when you strive and work hard for a goal. I will always tell them not to say 'I can't do it' and instead to say 'I WILL do it.' If they fail, at least they tried."

Nine months of perseverance, tears shed and fears overcome, paid off for Karen. She graduated in November 2003 with Honors. She landed an apprentice job immediately. Her greatest accomplishment came in February 2004 when she became self-employed. She named the business, after her father (her hero), Kennedy Electric and Cabling.

Karen has achieved her dream of becoming a successful business owner and a mentor for other women. "I want them to look at me and see it is possible to have big dreams, even when you feel that there is no hope." Her new career opened the door to her desire to teach. She is now the instructor for a practical electrical program for English as a Second Language adults at the Centre of Skills and Development Training in Burlington, Ontario, two days a week. She is very excited about this program.

Karen's sage advice to women is: "Believe in yourself. It can happen for you. Keep positive, laugh and smile everyday. When you come from the bottom of the pit, the only way is up, so take a chance and stop making excuses about why you can't try it out. If you want it, *go and get it!*"

Karen Hatcher, Burlington, Ontario.

This contribution, ©2005-2006, is used with permission.

Impress your family, friends and neighbors and have Karen Hatcher of Kennedy Electric and Cabling do all your electrical work. You may be pleasantly surprised that what has traditionally been a man's job can be done as well or better with a women's touch. Call 1-905-308-4567 or e-mail kelectric_cabling@sympatico.ca

Unconventional Careers

When thinking about a career, try thinking out of the box. I met one woman who was the first female funeral director in Canada. Another woman I met was a firefighter. Women in trades are becoming more common, although it is still a male-dominated field. If you have an aptitude for the skilled trades, it is an area worth exploring because it provides good financial benefits.

Think about being a clown, doggie masseuse, ghostwriter, singer of telegrams, pet detective (finding lost pets), flavorist (tastes food flavorings), headline writer for news…you get the idea! *See Resources at the end of this book for other creative employment ideas.*

Chapter 23

The Battle of the Same Sex:
Stay-at-home Mom vs. Working Mom

There is an uneasy standoff between the two kinds of mother,
which sometimes makes it hard for us to talk to each other. I
suspect that the non-working mother looks at the working mother
with envy and fear because she thinks that the working mum has
got away with it, and the working mum looks back with fear
and envy because she knows that she has not. In order to keep
going in either role, you have to convince yourself that the alter-
native is bad.

    I Don't Know How She Does It—The Life of Kate Reddy,
    *Working Mothe*r, a novel by Allison Pearson, Anchor
    Books, A Division of Random House Inc., 2002

We always want what the other person has. This book has been
about women getting back into the workplace after an extended
absence or as a result of changing careers in mid-life. But, what about
women who want to stay home? How do they square off with
working mothers? The tension felt between some of the stay-at-home
mothers and working mothers is often palpable.

    My husband and I were at his client's home for dinner. My children
were young at the time. The wife, a psychologist, asked me what I did.
Taking a deep breath, because I always felt uncomfortable with the
question—as if I was being interrogated or as if the essence of who I

was had to do with the kind of pay I was earning, I answered politely, "I am a stay-at-home mom." I felt I had to justify my position. Her response was "Oh," as in "that is too bad." Suddenly she was speechless. What could she possibly find to talk to me about now that our worlds were oceans apart? Maybe I was the only woman she knew who was not in the workplace. At least that was my perception. When she regained her ability to speak, she remarked, "As people are dying, the last thing they say is more likely to be 'I wish I had spent more time with my family' not 'I wish I had spent more time in the office.' It is good that you stay at home with your children." She was merely polite with me for the rest of the evening. Conversation had virtually dried up.

Other women spoke candidly of the uneasiness they feel around working mothers:

"I hate the feeling that I will be more accepted by my friends if I go back to work. Some of my working friends seem to have the idea that I have nothing to do all day—that I send my kids off to school and then watch TV until I have to pick them up. I realize my friends have to balance housework, childcare and their jobs. I don't envy what they have to do. I work very hard at what I do. I take care of my house, my kids, their pets, and stay on top of my volunteer commitments. I get everyone to school, activities and appointments. My family sits down together for meals, spends quality family time on weekends and has strong ties with extended family and friends at home and in other provinces."

Linda, 41, Winnipeg, Manitoba.

This contribution, ©2005-2006, is used with permission.

"When I wasn't working, family members and society looked down on me as if I were a useless person, who had no ambition or potential. My mother valued my staying home and felt that I was doing the best that I could do for my children."

F, 46, Thornhill, Ontario.

This contribution, ©2005-2006, is used with permission.

I asked working mothers:

1.   How do you perceive mothers who stay at home?
2.   Do you believe that you are more valued in society than full-time homemakers?

The following story is from a woman who wished to remain anonymous:

Her dream was to be a singer. Her parents were old-fashioned and they did not look upon such a career as worthy. So, like most women of her time (she is now 52), she bowed to the pressure of what was acceptable and became a daycare worker.

For over a quarter of a century, she has nurtured other people's children. Perhaps it would have been more agreeable to her if she did not have a special needs child of her own, whom she had to leave in the care of someone else while she tended to the children of her workplace. "There was guilt at times, especially when my daughter was younger. I felt that I was giving more to the other children than her, particularly if I was working with children who also had special needs. It was stressful if I had to leave her in another person's care when she was ill."

She has a mixed opinion on mothers who stay home with their children. "Sometimes I am envious or resent them. Other times I perceive that they don't do very much. In the end, I guess I respect women who nurture their children and wish I could have done the same."

She believes that she is more valued as a working mother, but she cautions that in her industry the value is only slightly higher. "I am viewed by the public as an overpaid babysitter. They have no idea what I do or how hard I work."

The years of lifting children have taken a toll on her. She suffers back problems and her hours have been cut back. She will probably be moved into a different, less strenuous situation. The uncertainty makes her uncomfortable. She has been doing this work so long that she is burnt-out. However, it is a comfort zone with security, a good pension and seniority. If she leaves, she will lose all that. She would love to get out of the industry and do something completely different, but like her stay-at-home peers trying to get back into the workplace, she lacks confidence in her ability to transition.

Janet, a working mother, states it succinctly: "I believe everyone should have a choice. I learned many years ago (when our son was young he presented us with many challenges that subsequently caused me to experience a lot of stress) not to criticize what another person does. We all do things for different reasons; what works for one doesn't necessarily work for another." What a refreshing point of view.

Janet, registered nurse/entrepreneur, 56, Toronto, Ontario.
This contribution, ©2005-2006, is used with permission.

The day that I sent the manuscript for this book to the publisher was also ironically the last day that I had to do the car pool—*ever*. My daughter is older, but because of bus complications, she could not take the bus to school, so I was in a car pool. I wrote the following poem about car pools which I dedicate to all the moms (and dads— my husband took his turns too) who has to do the grind of car pools:

No More Car Pool, No More Books, No More Children's Dirty Looks

After almost two decades,
I am free at last
from the responsibility
of my car pool task.

I have endured:
bites and fights,
reams of schemes,

lovers and leavers,
and children with dreams.

World travelers and talkers,
and silent ones too,
dawdlers and dodgers,
and thank you's—very few.

Tight parking spaces,
rushing around,
papers and mittens,
lost and found.

Sometimes forgetting
my car pool day,
mothers would phone me—
no wonder I'm gray!

In all kinds of weather,
rain or shine,
wanting and wishing for
some personal time.

I met rude people,
and new friends too,
waiting for my
motley crew.

For better or worse
I was a car pool mom.
Maybe that explains
why I'm so glum.

An era is over.

Now, what will I do?

WAIT

I see a light shining…

I will wear a new shoe:

Liberated woman free from the bonds of eternal car pool!

Chapter 24

Creating Employment When There Is None

If Bono and Bob Geldof were to rule the world, it may be a wilder and crazy place to live, but at least we would be debt-free and maybe even prosperous. Children would not be starving, everyone would have jobs and we would be having a rocking good time. Somehow the message of "We Are the World" (the recording made January 28, 1985, to raise money for Africa, made notable for its illustrious roster of performers, including Quincy Jones, Lionel Ritchie, Michael Jackson and Dionne Warwick), has been lost. Yes, we recently had the Live 8 concert to highlight the problem of global poverty and to try and eliminate it. I am absolutely for helping other countries and I am sympathetic to their plight; however, we also have to look after our own. These one-day feelings of warm and fuzzy and making the world a better place don't extend far enough into our everyday reality.

Across North America, there are many remote towns and villages where the only employer has closed their doors, or where the only employment opportunity involved industries, such as fishing or mining, which are no longer viable. And, let us not forget aboriginal communities and inner cities, where employment barely exits. It seems that being a contributing member of society is a hard-to-come-by option for many. The results are poverty, substance abuse and crime.

I met up with a dear First Nations Cree (that is what she likes to refer to herself as) woman last year. I have known her for years, but our lives keep going separate ways. She is in her early fifties, spent her young years in a forced Christian native school and comes from James Bay, Quebec, where hydroelectricity has only been available for the last 20 years or so. Her community still struggles for basic necessities that we all take for granted. Nevertheless, she is not bitter. Her enthusiasm and entrenched desire to make a difference is profound. She has completed her Masters in Education, knowing that education is the key to change. I told her about this project and she was excited by the prospect that I was trying to help women be employed.

She spoke of the many young mothers in her community who did not have full-time work. Many of these young women act as social workers and medical assistants without training, working in a clinic providing home care for the elderly. The only other rare opportunities for them are working in the band office or police/fire department doing secretarial work, at the one radio and television station nearby, or at the few stores or restaurants in town. A select few are trained to do native crafts. Cree culture believed in division of labor, but now the male leaders have a problem with women working with them. My friend is vying for the position of Band Leader. Her world will, indeed, change for the better if that is in the cards.

We discussed ideas on how we could create employment in areas where employment barely exists. The governments at all levels and other investors have tried to establish joint ventures. Things are moving at a snail's pace. A new clinic is being built. They are trying to improve educational opportunities generally. My friend is in the process of setting up a museum of her community's past and present. "It is important for the young people to know about our culture, to respect, be proud of it and to make it better," she says with conviction.

With the backing and support of a university professor, she has received funds to set up her project and to hire two women: one as a Development Officer to maintain, collect, document and arrange exhibits, and one elder to give advice. My friend will oversee the facility.

It is her hope that the artifacts, the oral recordings, photographs and research material will also attract tourists and researchers to the area.

My friend has also asked for another research grant to develop a plan for protecting the area's natural environment. Other ideas that are in the planning stage for the community include:

- food self-sustainment (presently fruits, vegetables and grains have to be brought in from Montreal);
- a filtration system for the rainwater;
- tapping into water from pure springs for bottling;
- fishing camps in the summer for tourists;

Within a few minutes, she and I came up with other possibilities, including:

- ecotourism (being careful not to damage the environment);
- ecolumber industry—using the lumber cautiously without destroying the forests (young people in her community have taken courses on carpentry and related trades, but have done nothing with it) for making such things as pre-fabricated log homes;
- wild berry farms—canning, preserving and selling the products;
- canoe factories and paddle making;
- moss use—ecofriendly diapers, and as compost;
- snowshoe making and tools;
- sewing hides, needlepoint and crocheting crafts and clothing for sale.

Since governments seem not to be able to make these things happen and government support services are sorely lacking, women will have to create their own work initiatives by making applications for the following funding options. These suggestions would apply to both small villages, such as the one mentioned above, or inner cities.

- Canada Proposals for Grants and Contributions. Interested and qualified applicants who have a project proposal can submit an application for funding to "carry out activities that meet a community need identified by HRSDC." Applications can also be made to set up a Business Resource Center—providing tools for setting up self-employment and career and employability programs (to help women find their passions, do resumes and learn job search techniques) for those that want to venture away from home.

- U.S.—HUD—Department of Housing and Urban Development and USDA Rural Development—Home of the Rural Empowerment Zone & Enterprise Community Program. *See more options and contacts in the Resources section of this book.*

The following are three additional options for creating employment funding for women:

1. For the last decade, micro financing has been gaining ground as an innovative approach to lending money. Small amounts of money by private lenders (usually non-profit agencies) are lent to poor communities to create their own opportunities for financial independence. These organizations are not about forgiving the debt. The borrowers are expected to pay back the funds with interest, and when they do, they are allowed to borrow larger amounts. This concept has mostly taken hold in Third World countries. It is slowly starting to be used in North America for small businesses requiring funds, when a larger bank will not lend them the money.

2. The National Business Incubation Association helps fledgling businesses set up in affordable rental areas. They provide shared services and office equipment, access to capital, business counseling and planning.

3. This last suggestion is the ancient custom of bartering: the exchange of goods and services.

As women, we can no longer sit back and wait for the help to come to us. We must be proactive. We can change the world and make it a better place!

Chapter 25

Mentoring and Coaching

A mentor can be defined as "someone who wants you to succeed and has the interest and time to devote to you."

"One thing I stress is that as you are inventing yourself, you need to have the larger good in mind. You need to be looking for ways to expand your circle of concern, looking for ways to mentor others.... This notion that we can put in our time on the home front and hit our stride in our forties is outrageous. We need to be giving back now. Finding some meaning through service."

Carolina Fernandez, author of ROCKET MOM! 7 Strategies to Blast You Into
Brilliance, Ridgefield, Connecticut, www.rocketmom.com e-mail emomrx@yahoo.com
or call 1-203 438-7164 "where brainy meets zany."
This contribution, ©2005-2006, is used with permission.

"The best mentor is not necessarily the most outwardly successful person you can find in your field. It's the one who will tell you what you need (not want) to hear and whose values are similar to yours. First, find someone you admire, then see if they qualify to mentor in your field."

Leslie Godwin, MFCC career & life transition coach, writer, speaker, author of
From Burned Out to Fired Up: A Women's Guide to Rekindling the Passion and
Meaning in Work and Life, *published by HCI Books, www.lesliegodwin.com*
e-mail lesliegodwin@lesliegodwin.com or call 1-818-880-4486 fax 1-818-634-4486.
This contribution, ©2005-2006, is used with permission.

The following contribution on coaching comes from Jill Crossland in Edmonton, Alberta:

There are times in our life when we realize that the next stage, transition or long-desired goal cannot be successfully achieved alone. When the advice from family and friends, no matter how caring, is not helping, that is the time to seek out a coach.

A coach is a trained professional who, simply put, 'partners with you at a certain point in your life to help you achieve a desired result.' The reasons that someone hires a coach are individual and varied. In today's busy and often overwhelming world, working with a coach is not a luxury but an efficient means to an end. Coaching sessions are designed to provide thought-provoking conversation, to hone in on what is and isn't working, to support, challenge, offer resources and guide the client toward their desired results.

For a woman who is about to re-enter the workplace, having a coach by your side could prove invaluable. Together you will explore your skills, look at who you are and examine the value that you can bring to the workplace.

A career coach's services may include:

- guiding you through the transition by bringing you up-to-date on today's workplace—how things have changed and what you can expect;
- preparation of resume and cover letter;
- working with you to update your image and marketable skills;
- providing networking tips;
- helping you to balance time and finances as you look for work;
- assisting you in preparing for the interview process.

Some coaches provide skills assessment and profiling. The person you hire will be a combination of training, plus their previous life and professional experiences. To find a qualified coach use these organizations:

International Coach Federation: www.coachfederation.org
International Association of Coaches: www.certifiedcoach.org

Choose three or four coaches from their referral service who meet
your criteria. Visit their Web sites, if they have one. There, you should
find a page that outlines their services and a biographical page. Most
coaches offer a free initial session that enables you to ask questions
and get a feel for how well you communicate with each other.

When hiring a coach, their fees should be within your budget, plus
you should feel that you have connected. Price per hour is not regu-
lated, so it varies. Coaches will offer sessions in office or by telephone
with e-mail support. A coach's job is not to provide all the answers;
you have to be committed to work toward your ultimate goal. Your
coach is going to bring out the best in you, and challenge and nudge
you to think about yourself in new ways and to perhaps consider
career choices that you may not have thought of before.

This contribution, ©2005-2006, is used with permission.

Jill Crossland is a life coach. Her company, Time Finders Coaching, specializes in working with and
for women. To learn more about Jill's services, her company and to read her on-line coaching
magazine for women, visit www.timefinderscoaching.net. E-mail jill@timefinderscoaching.net or
call toll-free 1-800-340-4412 or 1-403-901-6147.

Chapter 26

Success

If you live in a city, the roads are constantly under repair for potholes and cracks, and the highways are forever being widened. If you live in the country, the roads are winding, hilly and gravely; you can make the wrong turn and get lost. Wherever you live, the roads before you are the roads you have to take, but you *can* choose particular routes to travel that may be less difficult. The road is a metaphor for life.

All of the women in this book have endured bumpy roads. They anticipate that there will still be more in store ahead of them. They know they will have to stop at stop signs and lights, be held up in traffic, be housebound because of bad weather, and even that danger on the road can delay their journey. Their experiences in life have prepared them well. To the best of their ability, they will get back on the road to get to their destination.

These amazing women are a resounding success. They overcame hurdles, and in the process formulated a vision for themselves as self-sufficient, contributing members of society. The road of life has helped them change and grow. Their worlds are becoming richer, more meaningful. Some are even having fun in their transition. Many now share the lessons of their journey with others. As Gloria Stalarow, 58, of Houston, Texas, says, "Success is when you can pass it on to others." Gloria is the author of the soon-to-be-released book *Life After the Big 'D' and I Don't Mean Dallas: Eight Chapters of Surviving Divorce.*

Success is in the eye of the beholder. It does not mean that you have to be a Fortune 500 CEO making millions. Nor does it mean that you have to go for a Ph.D. Anything you have achieved that makes you happy and self-fulfilled can be defined as success.

I met a woman who had been a stay-at-home mom for 15 years. She was one of the lucky ones whose husband was able to provide a good living. When her children were teenagers, she decided she needed something for herself. "There are only so many years I can have lunch with the ladies, shop the malls and all the other trivial things that I did to fill up time while my kids were in school." She found a part-time job in a linen store. She is content. "It gives me a place to go that is flexible. I enjoy interacting with the customers and learning new things. I get along with my boss and I have a bit of spending money. What more do I need?"

Think of this time as a gift. You are older, more mature. It is a time to explore the possibilities and follow your heart's desire. Never be afraid to take risks. It is like love—it is better to have tried and failed than to never have tried at all. There is no greater feeling to boost your self-esteem than to see the fruits of your labor come to fruition!

My favorite motivational book is from the famous Dr. Seuss: *Oh, the Places You'll Go!* The book, released two years before the author died at age 87, was his last and most profound. It is quoted at graduating ceremonies around the world. In his simple, ingenious way of expressing himself, using fun words and colorful, exaggerated pictures, Dr. Seuss talks about the roads and paths that we travel to find success. Roads that are sometimes lonely, scary, confusing, long and difficult. Roads that make us uncomfortable, even dead-end roads. Being an optimist, however, he concludes by telling us about the joy, fun and knowledge we will find on the roads. If we never give up, success is almost certainly waiting at the end of the road.

Chapter 27

What's in It for Me? (WIIFM)

*I can be most helpful to people by creating words that will
compel people to react and make positive, effective changes.*
Heather Resnick

As the women and I sat around the table on our final day of the
Focus Program, we each had to describe why it was important that we
find employment. No matter what our backgrounds were, all of us felt
a need to contribute to the family coffers (out of necessity or obliga-
tion) and to society as a whole. Each of us desired to find a sense of
purpose for ourselves. There was not a dry eye among us.

We also had to put down one thing positive about each other on a
piece of paper. What the women had said about me opened up the
floodgates, prompting a group hug. They saw in me the courage that I
lacked and wisdom I never knew I had. They believed that I would
succeed as a writer. I said the words quoted above in June 2003—
before I knew that I would write this book. The proof of the power of
those words is now in your hands as you read *Women Reworked.*

We were a group of women who had never met before, sharing a
bond of fear of going back into the workplace. By the end of the two
weeks, we were confident that we would make our contribution to
the world. As a parting thank you to the women who shared my
challenges, I wrote a poem for them:

To My Focus Group

We were in the same boat two weeks ago.
We weren't quite sure, we felt kind of low.
We had no clue what we would do,
but Marla helped to see us through.
Somewhere in the process we all began
to see each other as a helping hand.
It's amazing to me how women can bond;
we help each other, we make us strong.
Our lives our busy, we usually move on,
but I think it would be great if we continued the bond.
Once a month we should get together;
it will help us all feel better.
I am grateful to all of you
for making me so positively new.
I wish you all health and success.
I believe in you to be the best!

Many women have a tendency to focus on everyone else around them and their needs, forgetting themselves in the process. This was evident to me from my interviews, from reading extensively and from conversing with other women. No matter what we do for others, we somehow feel that we are unworthy of praise and incompetent at creating a prosperous, fulfilling life for ourselves.

It was important for me to know and for the women to express what benefit they would derive from following their dream or their life's purpose. So I asked the question: "What's in it for you?" The question made them realize their growth and recognize their capabilities. It helped them replace panic with pride. The following are some of the responses I received.

"I lost my job three times in my career. A new job contributed to updating computer skills. The next job I acquired was that of a job developer. I loved helping others seek new employment, and being able to share what I went through during the time without a job. From there, I entered graduate school and have not stopped since. I am embarking on what I want to do when I grow up as a professional speaker and author."

Wilma J. Brown, 50+, Houston, Texas.
This contribution, © 2005-2006, is used with permission.

"I find this journey of self-employment exciting, but many times scary too, because I wonder if it could turn into a full-time job that will be enough to support myself and my son. Now, even with the unknown situations and difficulties, it is something I am finding very joyful and rewarding."

Claribel Angulo, The Giving Niche (design, crafts and art), 1-416-532-4385,
Toronto, Ontario.
This contribution, © 2005-2006, is used with permission.

"I am finding that by following true inspiration and keeping a positive attitude, it is possible to make dreams come true. I feel uplifted and free to try my wings, and I love the sheer joy of stretching and challenging myself…. If you face a decision between doing what feels safe, or making a big leap into following your heart's desire into the unknown—I encourage you to make that leap. It's scary to feel the ground slip under your feet, but when you're doing what you truly love, you'll find you've got wings and you're flying."

Cynthia Sue Larson, Berkley, California
This contribution, ©2005-2006, is used with permission.

Cynthia Sue Larson is the author of *Aura Advantage: How the Colors in Your Aura Can Help You Attain What You Desire and Attract Success,* and editor of *RealityShifter News* at http://realityshifters.com.

My own journey of self-discovery helped me mine my soul and recover a long-lost dream. I feel I am soaring now that I have found my purpose, my passion, my prize. As I reread my words and those of the beautiful women who contributed their heartfelt stories, it is my deep desire that they will inspire all women who are going through employment transitions and provide them power to make positive, effective changes in their life. There is no greater reward.

Chapter 28

Words From the Wise

All the women who contributed to this book are wise and inspiring. The following are some special samples of their wisdom:

"The only person that controls our destiny is ourselves."

Gloria Stalarow, 58, Houston Texas.

This contribution,©2005-2006, is used with permission.

Gloria is the author of the soon-to-be-released book, *Life After the Big 'D' and I Don't Mean Dallas: Eight Chapters of Surviving Divorce.*

"Women don't think they can offer the world of work much, when it's actually amazing how many skills they have acquired being home."

Val Nicholls, Vancouver Island, British Columbia.

This contribution, ©2005-2006, is used with permission.

"Everyone said that I couldn't start my own business with the idea of staying home with my son. I said they were wrong. I had to modify my work schedule around my son, but that is one of the decisions that has to be made when having a child and a business as a single parent. Fortunately, I am able to work from home, so I can allow myself to work at the times that work for me. Sometimes I paid for the all-nighters, but that's how things worked. My son is the reason I am doing this. Four years later, I continue to work around his schedule, but now I work while he's at school instead of pulling all-nighters. I have learned to set boundaries when it comes to family time and work time. I rarely cross these boundaries."

Manisha Solomon. This contribution, ©2005-2006, is used with permission.

Manisha's business, Solotext Editorial, specializes in book producing services for self-publishing authors. It offers "innovative and resourceful solutions for the problems authors face when undertaking the process on their own." www.solotext.com

"There are many resources to look into regarding overseas employment opportunities. My advice to your readers includes securing a position before leaving and having the work visa (which the company arranges) in hand before arriving. Also in the job offer, make sure the company provides a relocation package. You can check out www.Monster.com for research. Click on their international sites link and click on any country. They also offer background information and advice for each place of interest."

Mari, U.S. This contribution, ©2005-2006, is used with permission.

"Don't compromise. I moved forward by asking, 'If I was committed to thriving in my ideal life, what would I be doing?' I decided to see life as if (and repeat daily), 'This is my best year yet.' And I wrote a personal operating statement, which I repeated obsessively: 'Act with Integrity; Be of Good Cheer; Do Good; Walk Far.' When written, one mile was a challenge. Now I can travel 25 miles at an elevation of 9,000 feet along the Tahoe Rim Trail—in one day. Walk far became a metaphor."

Anne Lazarus, Reno, Nevada. This contribution, ©2005-2006, is used with permission.

Anne's business is SpringBoardInk, "Providing MOMENTUM to THRIVE for organizations and professionals." Communications development, strategic planning, coaching, workshops, training and keynotes. Springboardink@aol.com, 1-775-852-4973.

"Write a mission statement or at least do some soul searching before choosing your re-entry career. Keep in mind your skills, talents and, most of all, your calling. Don't waste valuable time and resources trying to fit into a job that isn't meaningful or satisfying to you. Take a 'day job' (one that allows you to pursue your true career path while bringing in needed income) but don't give up your calling."

Leslie Godwin. This contribution, ©2005-2006, is used with permission.

Leslie is an MFCC career and life transition coach, writer, speaker and author of *From Burned Out to Fired Up: A Women's Guide to Rekindling the Passion and Meaning in Work and Life,* published by HCI Books, www.lesliegodwin.com, e-mail lesliegodwin@lesliegodwin.com or call 1-818-880-4486/ fax 1-818-634-4486.

"I felt empowered when I started meditating regularly and began to recognize and understand my own behavioral patterns. In conjunction with journalizing, I manifested major changes in my life and still continue to reach higher."

Tammy Karaim, Erin, Ontario.

This contribution, ©2005-2006, is used with permission.

Tammy is a motivational speaker. Her business is Inner Lights, e-mail tkaraim@symptico.ca

"Women need to believe in themselves and go after what they want, regardless of the odds. Returning to work can seem scary, and being away from the workforce can lower self-confidence for many women. Don't let that deter you! It may sound trite, but I firmly believe that if you really want something and are willing to do a little homework, you can do anything. Thoughts really are 'things,' and if you fill your mind with nothing but positive self-talk and 'picture your success,' you will succeed."

Jan Brickman, U.S. This contribution, ©2005-2006, is used with permission.

Index

For further reference, *see also* List of Terms You Should Know for Job Searching on pages 177-180, and extensive **Resources/Bibliography** section on pages 181-198, which references Canadian and U.S. sources of information, including Web sites and books. Listings in Resources/Bibliography section are categorized by the following main topics:

List of Terms You Should Know for Job Searching

Specific programs vary regionally and locally. The more you know what services you require, the easier your job search. If you were to phone for help it would be better if you could be specific about your needs. For example, "I have been out of the workplace for over a year and I would like a job. I am not collecting any kind of employment insurance. Would you please tell me where I can go to get assessed." Whatever your ethnic origin, it is important to state that also, because their may be special services available to you.

A

Aboriginal/Native – Employment Services for Aboriginal/ First Nations People

Abused Women – Employment Services for Abused Women Entering the Workforce

Agricultural Programs

Apprenticeships – On the job-training program where you are being paid, usually for a skilled trade and you take an examination to be accredited in that field

Assessments, self (career) – Determining where your skills/passions lie. Government Assessments (usually free) or you can go to a paid professional career counselor

B

Business Development Bank of Canada for financing

Business Resource Centre – Offers assistance if unemployed and want to start your own business. Services include seminars, workshops, resources, consultation with business coaches and business registration

C

Career Counseling – Trained professionals who help you determine a career and the path to take

Career One Stop U.S. Dept of Labor

Career Planning

Coaching/Mentoring – A more experienced person in a company or organization who takes you under their wing. You can also pay private coaches

D

Dress for Success – non profit women's employment center. Helps you with employment dress advice. Term used to dress appropriately for interviews and on the job

Disability Learning, physical or mental

E

Education Funding – Funds to help you pay for formal education training

Employment for Disabled

Employment Insurance Claimants (EI) – 1-800-206-7218 Process to get back to work if you collect EI

Employment Resource Center – gives you the tools to conduct a job search. It is self-directed—you are given the resources: staff access, workshops, Internet access, phone, fax, computer services and a resource library so you can search for work at your own pace

English/French as a Second Language

F
Foreign Workers

G
Grants and Funding

H
Hidden Job Market Jobs that are not advertised in newspapers, for example. Almost 80% of jobs are found by networking or cold calling

Human Resources Skills Development Canada (HRSDC) provides funds for employment services and programs in Canada. HRSDC partners with various regional organizations responsible for delivering these services/programs throughout their areas

Human Rights in Employment
Immigrant/Newcomers

I
Incubation funds – Helps small businesses find inexpensive rental properties and services

Information Interviews – Find out about careers by meeting with people working in the industry

Industry Canada – Strategies for Job Seekers. Helps build a strong knowledge-based economy

Internships – Usually provided to students or new graduates of colleges and universities to learn about a specific business or government operation

J
Job Banks – Electronic job postings
Job Developers – Work with other government programs, provide one-on-one client consultation, and connect them up with potential employers.

Job Fairs – This is a recent concept where many employers gather in one place for the public to access information about their companies and job possibilities. It will give you the opportunity to view many different companies all at once. Check newspapers and trade magazines

Job Finding Clubs- Provide you with labor market information, employment leads and information on how to find a job

Job Profiles – Kinds of jobs available
Job Search – Locate government and private-sector job databases, or the activity of looking for a job

Job Shadowing – When you follow an employee around and watch as they do their job to learn how to do the job

L
Labour Market Information – Finding information about current trends in employment, including who is hiring, kinds of jobs and salaries

Learning Disabilites
Legal Rights – Employment and Interview
Literacy Skills
Local/Municipal – Check under Employment Assistance Programs in the "blue pages" of your white phone directory or the Yellow Pages
- Check local newspapers in the want ads section for employment programs
- Check community bulletin boards for upcoming employment workshops

M

Marketing Yourself – How to make employers want you

Microfinancing. Small amounts of money by private lenders (usually non-profit agencies) are lent to poor communities to create their own opportunities to financial independence

Mock Interviews – Practicing interviewing and videotaping them

N

Networking Clubs – Building relationships with a broad base of people who can help you find suitable employment. You can join formal groups for a fee or you can create your own

Non-Profit organizations

O

Occupation Information – Descriptions of various occupations

On-the-Job Training – Learning while you are on the job

On-line Learning – At home, education from computer courses from accredited schools (pre- and post-secondary), associations or governments

P

Provincial/Territorial Governments –
In your phone directory (blue pages) you would check under any or all of these topics/Ministries:

- Community and Social Services
- Consumer and Business Services
- Education, Enterprise—Opportunity and Innovation
- Employment
- Information for your Province or Territory

- Labor
- Training and Apprenticeships
- Training, Colleges and Universities
- Victim Services

Places to check for employment services
Other places to check to see what employment services are available to you:

- Phone or visit your local Municipal Center to find out what employment programs are available and if they provide a free community services directory
- Local newspapers in the want ads section for employment programs
- Community bulletin boards for upcoming employment workshops
- Local United Way to see what employment services are available to you
- Local community centers
- local YMCAs
- Adult education in local schools or centers
- Religious institutions
- Many cities provide free employment newspapers and magazines. Check commercial areas or wherever newspaper boxes are to see if they have any
- Many programs are free or at minimum cost to qualified people

Proposals for grants and contributions

R

Rehabilitative Programs for Women Leaving the Penal System

Resumé Writing

S

Self-Study – Learning a skill or trade by yourself through a creative means, for example, reading, watching television, observation or experimentation

Skilled trades, For example, electrician or carpenter – Check Training and Apprenticeship in the blue pages of the telephone directory or contact Training, Colleges and Universities or the equivalent

Small Business Organizations

Self-Employment

Skills Upgrading

Social Insurance Number – Canada

Social Security Number – U.S.

Social Development Canada – Services for Equal Opportunity

Specialized Training – A program offered by employers or unions for workers to upgrade their skills.

T

Temporary Employment Agencies, Headhunters

Training and Apprenticeships

Training and Learning – Where to obtain information.

Transferable Skills – Any skill you have learned in life that you can use in any job.

Hard Skills – Includes computer knowledge and accounting, for example.

Soft Skills – Could include organizational or communication skills

Trends in Employment

U

U.S. Department of Labor, Womens Bureau

V

Volunteering – If you type in volunteering, job category and where you are, descriptions of positions available will come up. There is also other career advice on the site

- Check within your religion or culture to see what services are available
- Check local community volunteer centers listed in your telephone directory (Government or Community Service Pages) under Volunteer
- If you are interested in the non-profit industry and wish to pursue a career in it, check your preferred College or University to see if they offer credited/diploma/degree courses. This is a growing industry.

W

Women's Resource Centre – provides resources such as education, counseling, skill development

Women Work – The national network for Women's Employment in U.S. Empowers women to have economic self-sufficiency

Resources/Bibliography

It is not usually necessary to type in the http:// unless there is no www. This is done below because the Web site addresses (URLs) were taken directly from the Internet to avoid any error. At the time of publication, and to the best of our knowledge, the URLs and other information cited here are correct.

ABORIGINAL/NATIVE HELP

Canada

- **Aboriginal Business Service Network** http://www.cbsc.org/ *this Web site is very long. 1.Click on it. 2. Click English or French. 3. Click Entrepreneurial Communities. 4. Click Aboriginal Business. 5 Click whichever site you want under Aboriginal Business.
- **Aboriginal Canada Portal** – Everything from health, employment, women's issues http://www.aboriginalcanada.gc.ca/ e-mail ACP@inac.gc.ca
- **Native Women's Association of Canada** foster social, economic, cultural and political well being of First Nations and Mètis Women http://www.nwac-hq.org/about.htm e-mail reception@nwac-hq.org or call 1-613-722-3033/ fax 1-613-722-7687
- **Women In Leadership** offers motivational programs for aboriginal women, women in transition and younger women. http://www.womeninleadership.ca/programs3.php

U.S.

- **Native American Business Listings** http://www.nwac-hq.org/about.htm
- **Native American Organizations and Urban Indian Centers** – excellent comprehensive list http://www.nativeculturelinks.com/organizations.html
- **Native American Organizations** List http://www.afn.org/~native/orgnztns.htm
- **Small Business Notes** – Native American Small Business Resources http://www.smallbusinessnotes.com/interests/nativeamerican.html
- **U.S. and Canadian Government Index of Resources** –WWW Virtual Library American Indians http://www.hanksville.org/NAresources/indices/NAgov.html
- **U.S. Department of Health and Human Services,** Indian Health Services – Women's Health http://www.ihs.gov/MedicalPrograms/MCH/WH.asp e-mail feedback@ihs.gov

ADDICTIONS, MENTAL HEALTH

U.S.

- **Get Mental Help Inc**. – Mental Health Matters – Mental Health Support Center. Lists disorders, information, support, treatments, therapists. Search by state. http://www.mental-health-matters.com/support/index.php e-mail infor@mental-health-matters.com 1-425-402-6934

Canada

- **Public Health Agency of Canada**. Canadian Health Network. Lists health organizations across country. Information on all health issues and where to find help. http://www.canadian-health-network.ca/

BATTLE OF THE SAME SEX

Books

- **Bishop, Ginny**, *Tween Time, Over 52 FREE Ways to Save Your Kids From Consumerism*, Happy Life Press, Toll free 1-800-431-1579, 1-303-729-2332 P.O. Box 270556, Littleton, CO. 80127   http://www.tweentime.com/
- **Fernandez, Carolina** *Rocket Mom! 7 Strategies to Blast You into Brillance*, Toll-free – 1-888-476-2493/ 1-438-7164 Fax 1- 425-650-2457, PO Box 569, Ridgefield, CT. 06877, e-mail emomrx@yahoo.co, for e-zine go to http://carolinafernandez.com/ "where brainy meets zainy"
- **Foley, Jacqueline** *Flex Appeal: An Inspirational Guide To Flexible Work for Mothers*, Out of Our Minds Press. E-mail jacqueline@getflexappeal.com, http://www.getflexappeal.com/

Magazine

- ***Working Mother* magazine**, Working Mother Media, PO. Box 5239, Harlan, IA 51593-0739, 1-800-627 0690, http://www.workingmother.com/ click on subscriber services. Every October this magazine lists the 100 Best Companies for Working Mothers.

COMEDY

- **Joyce Kaye Comedy Enterprises**, 1-954-346-7418/ fax 1-954-344-0629, 6190 NW 98th Drive, Parkland, FL 33076, e-mail Joyce@JoyceKaye.com Web site http://www.joycekaye.com/
- **Read** how to become a Stand-up Comic http://www.fabjob.com/
- **Second City** for training, touring http://www.secondcity.com/
- **Talent Rock** creates national televised events for entertainers. Display your talents to over 100 top industry professionals. Access workshops, conferences and get advice. Gaylord Palms™ Resort and Convention Center, Florida. http://talentrock.com/

CREATING EMPLOYMENT

Canada

- **Proposals for Grants and Contributions** http://www.sdc.gc.ca/ (a. Click Programs and Services. b. Click Grants and Contributions. C. Click Calls for Proposal.) Interested and qualified applicants who have a project proposal can submit an application for funding to "carry out activities that meet a community need identified by HRSDC." Apply to set up either or both a Business Resource Center – provides tools for setting up self-employment and career and employability program (to help women learn their passions, do resumes and learn job search techniques for those that want to venture away from home.
- **The Small Business Consumer Center** http://cdn-loans.grants-loans.org/programs.php
- **Calmeadow** – http://www.calmeadow.com/

U.S.

- **HUD – Department of Housing and Urban Development**, http://www.hud.gov/ a. Click Grants under Working with HUD in red column on left or call 1-202-708-1112 TTY 1-202-708-1457

- **USDA Rural Development** – Home of the Rural Empowerment Zone & Enterprise Community Program http://www.ezec.gov/ a. Click What's New box. b. Click Notices of Funding Availability. E-mail feedback@ocdx.usda.gov
- **National Association of Women Business Owners** to find out about other credit and support programs. http://www.nawbo.org/cms/index.php?pid=76
- **Microfinancing — The U.S. Small Business Administration** Microloan Progam for Women contact http://www.eqmoney.com/index2.htm http://www.sba.gov/financing/sbaloan/microloans.html. To locate a micro loan intermediary in your area click on the highlighted section at the bottom

International (including North America)

- **The Grantsmanship Center** http://www.tgci.com/ For Canada a. Click on Funding Sources box on top. b. Click on International. c. Click on Canada. For U.S. a. Click on Funding Sources box on top. b. Click on Grant sources by state.
- **Applying for a Corporate Sponsored Grant** is another possibility. Try Funds Net Services.com http://www.fundsnetservices.com/women.htm
- **Other links for microfinance** http://www.microlending.de/
- **The National Business Incubation Association** http://www.nbia.org/ http://www.nbia.org/resource_center/index.php for Canada and each state click links to State and International Associations
- **To find a local barter exchange** contact the National Association of Trade Exchanges http://www.nate.org/directorydetail.asp?ID=477 or call 1-440-205-5378 fax 1-440-205-5379.

DE-STRESS ABOUT STRESS

- **Loretta LaRoche's** (the "Master of Mirth") CDs. She is an international stress-management consultant who pokes fun at all of life's quirks and quacks. Contact Hay House Inc. P.O. Box 5100, Carlsbad, Ca 92018-5100, toll-free **1-800-654-5126, 1-760-431-7695**. fax toll-free **1-800-650-5115. Fax 1-760-431-6948** http://www.hayhouse.com/ She also has DVD's which are hysterical to watch and you can send free greeting cards via the Internet.
- **Richard Simmons** DVD. http://www.richardsimmons.com/ Canada and U.S.
- **Raven Crow** instructional DVD and other media related products. For private or group lessons call 1-877-969-0109 toll free or in the Toronto area 416-207-0350. http://www.idreamstudios.com/

Book

- **Stern, Susan** *Awakening Your Life Skills* published by Capricorn Press. Susan Stern Seminars & Keynotes Suite 103 - 232 Heath Street West Toronto Ontario M5P 1N8 http://www.susansternseminars.com/ e-mail susan.stern@sympatico.ca or call 1-416-489-1277

CD
- "**Listen to Your Heart**" produced by Angelworks, e-mail music@angelworks.org, toll-free 1-888-JOYOUS7 (569-6877)

DRESS FOR SUCCESS
- **Picadilly Fashions** store locator go to: http://www.picadillyfashions.com/store_locater.html
- **Dress for Success Affiliation** – To find a location of http://www.dressforsuccess.org/where_we_are/affiliates.asp
- Suppose there is no affiliate Dress for Success near you. This could be an opportunity to start a career in fashion and help other women. Dress for Success will help you. http://www.dressforsuccess.org/where_we_are/startyourown.asp
- For appearance at an interview http://www.dressforsuccess.org/interview_tips/
- http://www.careerwomen.com/resources/resources_502.jsp
- **Washington State University** – specific advice on what to wear including http://amdt.wsu.edu/research/dti/Women_Tips.html samples with comments on whether it is appropriate http://amdt.wsu.edu/research/dti/Women.html
- **Inexpensive (or free – check with each agency) clothing** or to find out where you go check:

    Goodwill Industries. To locate a retail outlet near you http://locator.goodwill.org/
    Local United Way http://www.uwint.org/gppweb/region/regionhome.aspx?MID=142
    Local Salvation Army http://www2.salvationarmy.org/ihq/www_sa.nsf
    Start a clothing change exchange in your community. To find out how to organize one contact: Volunteer Programs at Norwhich University 1-802-485-2670 in Randolph, Vermont

FEAR
- **Exercise** that will help you with your fears. *Tools for Personal Growth Overcoming Fears*: Coping.org is a Public Service of James J. Messina, Ph.D. & Constance M. Messina, Ph.D., e-mail: jjmess@tampabay.rr.com ©1999-2005 James J. Messina, Ph.D. & Constance Messina, Ph.D http://www.coping.org/growth/fears.htm

Books
- **A wonderful, simple tale**, in a book that you can read in an hour that will help you deal with overcoming fear by Johnson, Spencer M.D. *Who Moved My Cheese*? G.P. Putnam's Sons, New York, 2002 http://www.whomovedmycheese.com/ **A recent, excellent book** that will help you deal with all your emotions related to job search and/or transition by Tallar, Grace (especially if there are language or cultural barriers) *Get Hired on Demand*, Creative Management Training, 2004 http://www.newcomersupplies.com/

GOLDEN YEARS/SENIORS

U.S.
- **American Association of Retired Persons (AARP)** – A national non-profit organization for people 50 and over to help ensure their well-being emotionally, physically and financially. Offers opportunities to get back into the workplace as viable members of society. http://www.aarp.org/

Canada
- **Canada - Jobs for Seniors** –Employment Enjoyment at 55+
  http://www.seniorsforjobs.com/
- **Canadian Association of Retired Persons (CARP)** http://www.carp.ca
- **Retired Worker Canada** for part-time, temporary or project work
  http://www.retiredworker.ca/
- **Seniors Canada On-line** to access information for seniors http://www.seniors.gc.ca/
- **Experience Works Senior Workforce Solutions** training and employment services for mature workers. http://www.experienceworks.org
- **Computers made easy for seniors** http://www.csuchico.edu/~csu/seniors/computing2.html
- **Senior Net** – On-line community education and access to computer technologies
  http://www.seniornet.org/php/default.php

Magazine
- ***Fortune Magazine,*** May 16, 2005 V. 151, No.10 had an interesting article called "50 and Fired" by John Helyar. If you are a Fortune.com subscriber, you can find the Best Companies for Employees Over 50 and take an interactive quiz: *How Solid is Your Career?*

Web site Canadian
- **50plus.com** http://www.50plus.com E-mail info@50plus.com

ILLNESS/CANCER

Canada
- **Canadian Cancer Society** http://www.cancer.ca, e-mail ccs@cancer.ca or call
  Information Specialist 1-888-939-3333
- **Canadian Breast** Cancer Network http://www.cbcn.ca/english/resdb.php?browse&9
- **Myhealth Canada** – Patients and Families Support Groups for all health related issues
  http://www.myhealthcanada.com/patient_support.html

U.S.
- **American Cancer Society** - http://www.cancer.org/docroot/home/index.asp or call
  1-800-227-2345 (in U.S. only)
- **Cancer Index** Listings of 98 organizations http://www.cancerindex.org/clinks6a.htm
- **Cancer News** Listings for support, education, testing
  http://www.cancernews.com/support.html
- **Community Health Improvement** – Lists resources for all health related issues

- **Gilda's Club Worldwide**. Honoring the late comedienne Gilda Radner. A place where people who have been touched by cancer can go for emotional and social support. http://www.gildasclub.org/ For a resource list http://www.gildasclub.orgresourcedirectory/ e-mail – info@gildasclub.org or call 1-888-445-3248/fax 1-917-303-0549 http://www.fahc.org/Health_Improvement/support.asp e-mail ResourceCenter@vtmednet.org http://www.y-me.org/
- **Oncochat** – Real time on-line peer support for ccancer survivors, families and friends http://www.oncochat.org/ e-mail rkherman@charter.net
- **Y-Me National Breast Cancer Organization** – Provides support, education

Books
- **Peltosaari, Leila**, *Dancing With Fear* Verdun, Quebec, Canada www.tikkabooks.com or leila@tikkabooks.com
- **Watters, Debbie, with Haydn and Emmett Watters, Photographs by Sophie Hogan,** Second Story Press, Toronto, 2005, *Where's Mom's Hair? A Family's Journey through Cancer.*

INTERVIEW SAVVY
Canada
- **Canada Human Rights** Know your legal rights http://www.chrc-ccdp.ca/publications/screening_employment-en.asp

U.S.
- **Find Law** for the Public Illegal Interview Questions Special Considerations for Women http://employment.findlaw.com/articles/2446.html
- **The American with Disabilities Act** http://www.eeoc.gov/facts/ada18.html
- **About InterviewTips** http://jobsearchtech.about.com/od/interview/l/blt_interviews.htm
- **Employment Law** (Grosman, Grosman and Gayle LLP) http://www.grosman.com/freelegalinfo/employmentlaw/emp03b.htm
- **Employment Law** (Spray, Gould and Bowers LLP) http://www.sgblaw.com/faq_emp.shtml#1
- **Monster.com** http://interview.monster.com/archives/attheinterview/
- **What to say about disclosing a disability** http://www.alis.gov.ab.ca/tips/archive.asp?EK=163

KNOWLEDGE IS POWER
Book
- **Alexander, Janet E. and Tate, Marsha Ann** , Lawrence Erlbaum Associates, 1999. *Web Wisdom: How to Evaluate and Create Information Quality on the Web*
- **Trends in the industry** To find out what industries are prolific, salaries, and so on. This is also known as Labor Market Information (LMI).

On-Line Book
- ***Making Career Sense*** *of Labor Market Information*
  http://www.makingcareersense.org/

Canada
- **Canada – Statistics Canada** http://142.206.72.67/r000_e.htm and click The Economy. It will give you the country's economic and social trends. *Statistics are constantly changing, so they will never be current.
- **Canada Yahoo HotJobs** http://ca.hotjobs.yahoo.com/jobseeker/company/company_volunteers_list.html A list of organizations that use volunteers.
- **Labor Market Information**http://www.labourmarketinformation.ca/

U.S.
- **Job Corps Career Development Resource Centre**
  http://www.jccdrc.org/oa/labormarket-acinet
- **U.S. Coolworks -** http://www.coolworks.com/volunteer
- **U.S. - U.S. Department of Labor, Bureau of Labor Statistics** http://stats.bls.gov/

Job Fairs
- Bayone.net http://www.bayone.net/eng/job-fairs.htm
- Career Fairs http://www.careerfairs.com/
- Expo Central.com http://www.expocentral.com/index.html
- National Job Fair and Training Expo Canada http://www.thenationaljobfair.com
- **Contractor City** - resource portal for women in the trades
  http://www.contractorcity.com/modules.php?name=WIC
- **Scholarships for women** in trades, technology and operations – National Association of Women in Contstruction http://www.nawic.org/reasonstojoin.htm or Edfinancial services Scholarship

LEARNING DISABILITIES
Canada
- **Learning Disability Association**, information, solutions and tools for any age.
  http://www.ldac-taac.ca/

U.S
- **Learning Disability Association of America**, information, solutions and tools for any age. To find a state chapter of http://www.ldanatl.org/
- **Learning Disability Institute LDI** is a national non-profit organization. For information, statistics and reports http://www.ldinstitute.org/idea97C.shtml
- **Attention Deficit Disorder(ADD)** General Information about http://add.about.com/
- **National Centre for Learning Disabilities** http://www.ld.org/# main page, for adults http://www.ld.org/livingwithld/adults_home.cfm

Book
- **Singer, Rhona Dr.** *How Antsy Pantsy Became Stone Woman Warrior.* Stone Woman Warrior Press, 2005. www.stonewomanwarrior.ca

On-LineArticles

- **Canada** http://www.ldac-taac.ca/ld%2Dlaw/
- **U.S**. http://www.eeoc.gov/types/ada.html
- **Articles and resources** for women with http://add.about.com/od/womenandadd/
- **Excellent article** on some of the issues women face if they have ADD. http://add.about.com/od/womenandadd/a/women.htm
- **LD is covered by law** in Canada and the U.S. Know your rights.

LOSING A LOVED ONE

- **Canada – The Grief Recovery Institute** http://www.grief.net/ St. William, Ontario e-mail info@grief.net or call 1-519-586-8825/ fax 1-519-586-8826
- **U.S.** Sherman Oaks, California, e-mail usinfo@grief.net or call 1-818-907-9600 fax 1-818-907-9329
- **U.S. National Grief Support List** http://www.thenewsongcenter.org/pages/ nationalgriefsupport.htm, e-mail info@thenewsongcenter.org
- **Yahoo Directory on Death and Dying Canadian Listings** http://ca.dir.yahoo.com/Regional/Countries/Canada/Society_and_Culture/Death_and_Dying/
- **Yahoo Directory on Death and Dying U.S. Listings** http://ca.dir.yahoo.com/Society_and_Culture/Death_and_Dying/?sort=lf
- **Bereavement Families Online** http://www.bereavedfamilies.net/index.html, e-mail admin.bfo@axxent.ca

MENTORING/COACHING
Coaches

- **Jill Crossland**, Time Finders Coaching, http://www.timefinderscoaching.net (on-line newsletter) e-mail jill@timefinderscoaching.net or call toll free 1-800-340-4412 or 1-403-901-6147, Edmonton, Alberta.
- **Anne Lazarus**, SpringBoardInk, Providing MOMENTUM to THRIVE for organizations & professionals. Communications Development>Strategic Planning>Coaching>Workshops>Training & Keynotes, Reno, Nevada. Springboardink@aol.com 1-775-852-4973
- **Alternative Coaching Lists** of practitioners Canada and U.S. http://business.cbel.com/alternative_coaching/
- **International Coach Federation**: http://www.coachfederation.org/eweb/
- **International Association of Coaches**: http://www.certifiedcoach.org/

NATURAL ALTERNATIVE HEALING
Coaches

- **Maureen Sherman** Certified Coach Wholistic Lifestyle Consultant "Soulworks" "The best is yet to be—Intention is the Key" 905-685-7235, e-mail Maureen@mergetel.com

- Reflexology Schools and Courses. Lists schools and organizations international http://www.healingfeats.com/rfschl.htm
- **Leslie Godwin**, MFCC Career & Life Transition Coach, Writer, Speaker, Author *From Burned Out to Fired Up: A Women's Guide to Rekindling the Passion and Meaning in Work and Life,* published by HCI Books http://www.lesliegodwin.com/e-mail lesliegodwin@lesliegodwin.com or call 1-818-880-4486/ fax 1-818-634-4486
- **Tammy Karaim**, Motivational Speaker, Inner Lights, e-mail tkaraim@symptico.ca Erin, Ontario
- **See above** for list of alternative coaches
- To become a WaveMaker Coach – Gets to the root of peoples problems using technology and training contact WaveMaker Coaching http://www.wavemakercoaching. com/about.html e-mail Info@InnerHumanDesign.com or call 1-619-557-2700

NETWORKING
- **Canadian Women's Business Network** www.cdnbizwomen.com
- **Connecting Women** www.ivillage.com/work/

Books:
- **Bolles, Richard** *What Color Is Your Parachute A Practical Manual for Job-Hunters and Career-Changers* Ten Speed Press Berkley, California, 2004 edition http://www.JobHuntersBible.com
- **Darling, Diane** *The Networking Survival Guide,* McGraw –Hill, New York, NY, 2003 http://www.makeyourwordscount.com e-mail info@makeyourwordscount.com 1-905-567-8454
- **Messer, Donna** *Effective Networking Strategies,* ConnectUs Communications Canada, Oakville, Ontario 1998) http://www.connectuscanada.com/ e-mail info@connectuscanada.com 1-905-337-9578 fax 1-905-337-9320
- **Zorn, Renate** *Good Conversation is for Everyone 10 Steps to Better Conversations,* Make Your Own Words Count, Mississauga, Ontario 2003 http://www.makeyourwordscount.com e-mail info@makeyourwordscount.com 1-905-567-8454
- **Zorn, Renate** *The Woman in the Red Dress and Nine Other Secrets of Networking Success,* Make Your Own Words Count, Mississauga, Ontario 2005

Newspaper
- ***Wall Street Journal*** – Tips on networking http://www.careerjournal.com/jobhunting/networking/
- **Lillian D. Bjorseth**, President Duoforce Enterprises, Inc. Speaker, Trainer, Author – Business Networking Business Development, Communication Skills http://www.duoforce.com e-mail lillian@duoforce.com Lisle, Illinois
- **Toastmasters Association**. I http://www.toastmasters.org/ e-mail toastmasters@xmr3.com

NEWCOMERS/IMMIGRANTS
Book
- **Tallar, Grace** *Get Hired On Demand*, for on-line career training and subscription to her newsletter, or to hire Grace as a speaker, contact at info@newcomersupplies.com, http://www.NewcomerSupplies.com, 905-726-8005.

Canada International
- Canada Site – Information for newcomers on finding a home, language training, employment, education, health, citizenship etc. http://www.canadainternational.gc.ca/ click Newcomers to Canada on left side under Services for e-mail Canada International@Canada.gc.ca or fax 1-613-941-1827 (charges may apply)
- **Citizenship and Immigrationship Canada** – Immigrating to Canada – All you need to know if you are thinking of moving here. Also information if you are already in Canada. http://www.cic.gc.ca/english/immigrate/ or call 1-888-242-2100 (Canada Only) For information on Permanent Resident Card (PR Card) 1-800-255-4541 (Canada Only) TTY 1-888-576-8502 (Canada Only)
- **Immigrationexpert.com** Canadian Jobs and Immigration http://www.immigrationexpert.com/ or call 1-416-488-9500 fax 1-416-480-9600

U.S.
- **Citizenship and Immigration Services** http://uscis.gov/graphics/ Lists important government numbers. National Customer Service Center (NCSC) TTY 1-800-767-1833
- **Canada U.S. Employment** – Helps find employment for people relocating to or temporarily residing in Canada or U.S. http://www.canadausemployment.com/ or call 1-800-600-4091 in North America /fax 1-800-868-9804, outside North America 1-416-636-3933/fax 1-416-636-8113

PRE-EMPLOYMENT
- **Focus** – a Career and Employability Workshop for women who have been out of the workplace for awhile and not collecting employment insurance. 1-905-737-9522 x348, Fax 1-905-883-6795 *This Program is only offered in York Region, Ontario. http://www.employmentsource.ca/
- **Breakthrough**, run by the Academy of Learning. *This Program is only offered in York Region, Ontario. E-mail aolrichmondhill1@rogers.com or call 1-905-508-5791 fax 1-905-508-9409.
- **Community MicroSkills Development Centre** Toronto [*only Toronto], ON Canada 416-247-7181 X201 (Employment Resource Centre) fax 416-247-1877 http://www.microskills.ca/
- **Human Resources Centre** – local, in your phone directory, look in the blue pages under the "Employment" section, subheading "Federal – Human Resource Centers" or call Information Government of Canada 1-800-622-6232. National HRSDC Web site http://www.hrsdc.gc.ca offers extensive employment, skills and labour market information.

English – http://www.hrsdc.gc.ca/en/gateways/nav/top_nav/our_offices.shtml
French – http://www.rhdcc.gc.ca/fr/accueil.shtml
English services where you live –
http://www.hrsdc.gc.ca/en/gateways/where_you_live/menu.shtml
French services where you live –
http://www.rhdcc.gc.ca/fr/passerelles/pres_de_chez_vous/menu.shtml

- **To get to Jobs, Workers, Training and Careers**, http://www.jobsetc.ca
- **For A-Z** listings of all the programs and services for HRSDC -
  http://www.hrsdc.gc.ca/en/gateways/nav/top_nav/azindex.shtml#l
- **Publications and reports** – http://canada.gc.ca/publications/publication_e.html
- **Social Development Canada** (SDC) – provides equal opportunity services for all
  Canadians http://www.sdc.gc.ca/en/gateways/where_you_live/menu.shtml
- **For A-Z listings** of all programs and services for SDC
  http://www.sdc.gc.ca/en/gateways/nav/top_nav/ps.shtml
- **Industry Canada Strategis for Job Seekers** – works with Canadians to build a
  growing, competitive knowledge-based economy
English http://strategis.ic.gc.ca/sc_x/engdoc/job_seekers.html?strategisfor=e_job
French http://strategis.ic.gc.ca/sc_x/frndoc/job_seekers.html

Province and Territory Sites:
http://canada.gc.ca/othergov/prov_e.html or www.nfld.net/eshn/government_sites.html

- **Canada's municipalities** links to the official Web sites of: http://www.munisource.org
- **U.S. – All Federal Government Services** – http://www.info.gov/toll-free.htm Call
  toll-free at 1-(800)-FED-INFO [1 (800) 333-4636] between 8 a.m. and 8 p.m. eastern time
  Monday through Friday, except Federal holidays or for the government blue pages
  http://www.usbluepages.gov/
- **U.S. Department of Labor Women's Bureau** – http://www.dol.gov/wb/
  To find programs and services near you. Click on your State on the map and an alphabet-
  ical State list will come up with the programs and services in that state.
  http://www.dol.gov/dol/location.htm
- **America's Job Bank** – http://www.ajb.dni.us/ Provides many career related topics and
  where to get help. It is a component of CareerOneStop – http://www.careeronestop.org/
  Post your resume, learn about job openings, and so on
- **For a service near you** http://www.servicelocator.org/
- **Women Work!** For a service location near you
  http://www.womenwork.org/resources/directory.htm (202) 467-6346
  fax (202) 467-5366 womenwork@womenwork.org Program Referral/Information
  Packet Request Line*: (800) 235-2732
- **Upgrading your education** and where you can get financial help
  http://www.womenwork.org/pdfresources/finaid.pdf

- *The toll-free number goes to a recording and requests are processed every few months. For inquiries needing immediate response, please call directly at (202) 467-6346 or contact by e-mail at womenwork@womenwork.org. To learn about education & job training programs in your community, please check online program directory.
- **Department of Labor** main Web site http://www.dol.gov/wb/
- **For training** http://www.dol.gov/dol/topic/training/index.htm
- **Free self-assessments** and other career information
  http://www.cdm.uwaterloo.ca/
  http://www.coun.uvic.ca/career/c-match.html
  http://www.jobfutures.ca/en/home.shtml
  http://careerplanning.about.com/
  http://www.assessment.com/

Other Career Resources:
- http://www.possibilitiesproject.com/index.asp
- http://static.jobtrak.com/job_search_tips/search.html

CD
- "**Getting the Job You Want and Keeping It**" – **Volume 1,** produced by Angelworks®
  E-mail info@gettingthejobyouwant.com

E-Book
- **Stephenson, Brian CTM, Tatum, Nicholas CTM** *Job Search Bootcamp: The Ultimate Course.* 2005 http://www.jobsearchbootcamp.com/
- **Overseas opportunities** http://english.monster.ca/geo/siteselection.asp for research. Click on their international sites link and click on any country. They also offer background information and advice for each place of interest.

Books
- **Bolles, Richard Nelson** *What Color Is Your Parachute: A Practical Manual for Job-Hunters & Career Changers*, Berkeley, CA: Ten Speed Press, 2004 (Updated yearly) it is a best-seller and a lot of fun to read! http://www.JobHuntersBible.com
- **Johnson, Tory, Freedman-Spizman, Robyn and Pollak, Lindsey** *Women For Hire: The Ultimate Guide to Getting a Job*, New York, New York. The Berkley Publishing Group, A division of Penguin Putnam, 2002. Geared for the 'just graduated' but most of the advice applies to all women. Excellent.
- **Johnson, Spenser** *Who Moved My Cheese? An Amazing Way to Deal with Change in Your Work and in Your Life.* New York, NY: Putnam, 2002. A simple little tale that helps you gather courage to move on in your life.
- **Watters, Marge,** *It's Your Move: A Personal and Practical Guide to Career Transition and Job Search for Canadian Managers, Professionals and Executives* HarperCollins Publishers Ltd., Toronto. 2004

Magazines

- **Worthwhile®** , dash30 Inc. 1201 Peachtree Street, Suite 1718, Atlanta, GA 30361, 404-872-9992, toll-free 1-888-385 6820 http://www.worthwhile.com/ e-mail info@worthwhilemag.com
- **Esteem Embracing Success**, P.O. Box 93554, Toronto, ON. Canada M4C 5R4, 416-724-3427, http://www.esteemagazine.com e-mail info@esteemagazine.com

PUBLISHING

- **International Women's Writing Guild** – Non-profit "network for the personal and professional empowerment of women through writing." http://www.iwwg.org/, e-mail iwwg@iwwg.org P.O. Box 810, Gracie Station, New York, NY 10028 212-737-7536 fax 212-737-9469
- **Creative Bound International Inc.** "Helping experts get their message out" http://www.creativebound.com/ e-mail info@creativebound.com
- **Barbara Florio Graham** – Book Publishing Consultant http://www.simonteakettle.com/
- **Manisha Solomon**, Solotext Editorial, http://www.solotext.com/. Book producing services for self-publishing authors: Innovative and resourceful solutions for the problems authors face when undertaking the process on their own.

Books

- **Anderson, Suzanne**, *Self Publishing in Canada,* Half Acre Publishing, Duncan, British Columbia, 2003
- **Page, Susan**, *The Shortest Distance Between You and a Published Book: 20 Steps to Success, Broadway Books, New York, NY, 1997*
- **Poynter, Dan**, T*he Self-Publishing Manual*, Para Publishing, Santa Barbara, California, 2003
- Ibid, *Successful NonFiction, Ibid*, 2000
- Ibid, *Writing NonFiction Turning Thoughts Into Books*, Ibid, 2000
- **Ross, Tom & Marilyn**, *The Complete Guide to Self-Publishing,* Writer's Digest Books, Cincinnati, Ohio, 2002

Marketing Your Books

- **Kremer, John**, *1001 Ways to Market Your Books,* Open Horizons, Fairfield, IA, 1998
- **Ross, Marilyn & Tom**, *Jump Start Your Book Sales,* Communication Creativity, Buena Vista, Colorado, 1999
- **Silverman, Francine**, *Book Marketing from A-Z,* Infinity Publishers.Com, West Conshohocken, PA, 2005

Free E- Newsletters

- **Poynter, Dan**, "*Publishing Poynters Newsletter*", http://ParaPub.com, e-mail DanPoynter@ParaPublishing.com
- **Stewart, Joan**, "*The Publicity Hound*", http://www.publicityhound.com/ e-mail JStewart@PublicityHound.com *Great information for any business!
- **Nominal Fee -** Silverman, Francine "*Book Promotion Newsletter*", http://www.bookpromotionnewsletter.com/ or http://www.nystatetravel.com/ , e-mail franalive@optonline.net

REHABILITATION FROM A PENAL INSTITUTION
Canada
- **Canadian Families and Corrections Network** (613) 541-0743
- **Correctional Services Canada** Community Release Programs and Support Sevices http://www.canada.gc.ca/ or call 1-800-622-6232 for your nearest Correctional Service Office.or http://www.csc-scc.gc.ca/text/contact_e.shtml E-mail: cfcn@sympatico.ca Web site: http://www3.sympatico.ca/cfcn/
- **The Elizabeth Fry Assocation** – http://www.elizabethfry.ca/caefs_e.htm e-mail caefs@web.ca call 1-613-238-2422

U.S.
- **Family and Corrections** Network Directory http://www.fcnetwork.org/Dir2004/dir2004al-fl.html
- **Women in Community Service (WICS)** http://www.wics.org/ They also offer a program called Lifeskills™ that helps women in the penal system prepare for employment and integration into the community. Toll-free – 1-800-442-9427, 1-703-671-0500 fax 1-703-671-4489

SELF-EMPLOYMENT
*Most of the women in this book are self employed. Please use the contact information (if available) at the bottom of each story.
Canada
- **Business Development Bank of Canada** http://www.bdc.ca/flash.htm?cookie%5Ftest=1 delivers financial and consulting services to Canadian small business including First Nations.
- **Canada – Small Business Canada** for a sample business plan http://sbinfocanada.about.com/cs/businessplans/a/bizplanoutline.htm
- **Canada – Women in a Home Office** is a Canadian organization that brings women together in monthly meetings, workshops and telemeetings to help women grow and get support in their home businesses. http://www.womeninahomeoffice.com/online.htm
- **Canada Business Service Centres** – To see a sample business plan from http://www.cbsc.org/ when you press English or French and the window opens up either type in words business plans or click business start-up. To find out your nearest business centre click Government services and programs on the left side and follow the prompts.
- **Canada One Sites for Canadian Women in Business Comprehensive Lists** http://www.canadaone.com/magazine/women.html
- **Canadian Careers resource list** http://www.canadiancareers.com/smallbusiness.html
- **Canadian Government Grants** http://www.businessguide.net/
- **Canadian-Ontario Business Service Centre (COBSC)** www.cbsc.org toll-free 1-800-567-2345
- **Home business ideas** http://www.mymommybiz.com http://www.hrsdc.gc.ca/en/gateways/nav/top_nav/our_offices.shtml

- **Local Human Resource Centre (now comes under the umbrella of Service Canada)** http://www.servicecanada.gc.ca/ , toll-free 1-800-622-6232) will be able to give you the nearest self-employment program; they will guide you through the process
- **Set-up, operating**, invigorating your business, networking, programs – go to http://www.entrewomen.ca/
- **Small Business Information Canada** – Articles and tips on marketing your business: http://sbinfocanada.about.com/cs/marketing/a/marktipsindex.htm
- To obtain **Guide for Canadian Small Business** from Canada Customs and Revenue Agency phone 1-800-959-2221 or http://www.cra-arc.gc.ca/
- **Women Entrepreneurs of Canada** http://www.wec.ca/index.php speakers and networking for women entrepreneurs

Magazine

- **Canada – Progressive Choices** (published in Dartmouth, Nova Scotia) is a magazine for Canadian Women in Business 1-888-232-3297
- **See** Pre-employment section for other magazines.

U.S.

- **Advancing Women's Business Centre** http://www.advancingwomen.com/business.html
- **Entrepreneur.com** http://www.entrepreneur.com/marketing/0,6994,,00.html http://ecircleu.com/articles.php Click Support for Entrepreneurs and Small Businesses http://ecircleu.com/show_article.php?id=42&pageNum_articles=1&totalRows_articles=33 . For samples of business plans http://www.bplans.com/dp/
- **Life Tools for Women** http://www.lifetoolsforwomen.com/links-money.htm
- **Powerful Proposals** http://www.proposalwriter.com/grants.html For women-run businesses http://www.proposalwriter.com/small.html.
- **SCORE Counselors to America's Small Business** http://www.score.org/ another valuable site. For business plan information http://www.score.org/template_gallery.html
- **U.S. – E Circle U** Power Tools for Starting and Running Your Own Busniness, this site is a jam-packed with free self-employment information.
- **U.S. On-line Women's Business Center** (Office of Women's Business Ownership, SBA) http://www.sba.gov/onlinewbc/. You can find your nearest Women's Business Center
- **U.S. Small Business Administration** http://www.sba.gov/
- **U.S. Small Business Funding Opportunities** http://grants.nih.gov/grants/funding/sbir.htm
- **Women in Business – Learnactivity.com** provides invaluable information for women entrepreneurs on organizations, Web sites, magazines and articles is http://www.learnativity.com/women.html
- **Women's News Bureau** Division of International Virtual Women's Chamber of Commerce – for women who run virtual businesses http://womensnewsbureau.com/
- **Women-21.gov** – ensures viability of women in business http://www.women-21.gov/

Books

- **Cobe, Patricia, and Parlapiano, Ellen H**. *"Mompreneurs": A Mother's Practical Step-By-Step Guide to Work-at-Home Success"* A Perigee book, The Berkley Publishing Group, division of Penguin Purnam Inc, New York, NY, 2002.
- **Edwards, Paul and Sarah**, *Finding Your Perfect Work: The New Career Guide to Making a Living, Creating a Life*, Jeremy P. Tarcher/Putnam, member of Penguin Putnam, New York, NY. 2003.
- **Friedman, Caitlin & Yorio, Kimberly**, *The Girl's Guide to Starting Your Own Business*, Harper Collins New York, NY, 2003.
- **McGuckin, Frances**, *Business for Beginners*, Eastleigh Publications, Langely, British Columbia, 2003.
- **Thomas Yaccato, Joanne with Jubinville, Paula**, *Raising Your Business: A Canadian women's guide to entrpreneurship,* Prentice Hall, A Division of Simon & Schuster, 2002.
- **Total Web International Net Consulting** – Consulting and Business Solutions http://www.totalweb-inc.com/
- **"Entrepreneur able"**, do the following on-line quizzes: http://www.wd.gc.ca/tools/xindex_e.asp http://www.liraz.com/webquiz.htm

SHOPPING-RELATED CAREERS

- **About Career Planning** http://careerplanning.about.com/cs/choosingacareer/a/hobby.htm
- **All Business Champions of Small Business** Informative articles, links to read about hobby-based businesses can be found at http://www.allbusiness.com/articles/content/3328-2057-1640.html
- **Learning Annex**. http://www.learningannex.com .Click on other cities to find the location closest to you for workshops related.
- **Mystery Shopper Coaches Corner** by Melanie Jordan before applying for a mystery job http://www.mysteryshoppercoach.com/mysteryshopperscams.html
- **Personal Shopper** – Fab Job.com They provide e-books on other exciting career possibilities, also http://www.fabjob.com/
- **Sharon's Shop at Home – Unique Giftware** by appointment only at 1-647-298-0112, fax 1-905-886-2477, e-mail rosh_ent@hotmail.com .
- **Starting up your own personal shopping** business can be found at http://www.iversonsoftware.com/success/1033.htm

TECHNOPHOBIA

Also check pre-employment above for computer courses and so on.

- **Industry Canada** – Community Access Program provides Internet and computer training programs that are offered locally. http://cap.ic.gc.ca/pub/index.html?iin.lang=en Web site in English and French
- **Webgrrls** – training, networking, support and careers for women in the technological fields http://www.webgrrls.com
- **Where you can obtain a computer** and how to get connected to the Internet. http://www.womenwork.org/pdfresources/internet101.pdf
- **Wired Women** (Canada) – encourages women in technology to build successful careers by supporting them with education, mentorship and networking opportunities. http://www.wiredwoman.com/mc/page.do
- **YourNameSells.com** building professional Web sites you control, http://www.yournamesells.com/
- **If you require funding for courses**, check your local employment service center (see above) to see how you can apply for financial assistance.

Professional Computer Courses

- In Canada check out CDI College. http://ca.college-info.org/&kid=OVR0002194455?OVRAW=cdi&OVKEY=cdi&OVMTC=standard
- In the United States check http://www.computertrainingschools.com
- **Examples of jobs that require computer skills**
Canada http://www.jobsetc.ca/category_drilldown.jsp?category_id=1158&crumb=1126&crumb=1158&lang=e
U.S.http://www.acinet.org/acinet/library_search.asp?Keyword=computers&id=14&nodeid=23&x=37&y=12

TEMPORARY EMPLOYMENT AGENCIES AND HEADHUNTERS

- http://www.jobsetc.ca/directory or various agencies
- http://www.jobsetc.ca/category_drilldown.jsp?category_id=435&lang=e

UNCONVENTIONAL CAREERS

- **Karen Hatcher, Electrician** of Kennedy Electric and Cabling for all your electrical work. You may be pleasantly surprised that a usual man's job done with a women's touch is of equal or greater value. 1-905-308-4567, e-mail kelectric_cabling@sympatico.ca
- **Canada – To find programs and services in a skilled trade** or any employment http://www.hrsdc.gc.ca/en/home.shtml
- **Back Door Jobs** If you are an adventurer and can spare time away from home, check out http://www.backdoorjobs.com/ for short-term job adventures.
- **Canada Inventive Woman** – If you have a great idea that you want to patent or develop contact http://www.inventivewomen.com

- **U.S. to find One Stop Career Center** in the. U.S. Department of Labor, Women's Bureau http://www.dol.gov/dol/topic/training/index.htm America's Service Locator 1-877-US2-JOBS (872-5637) (in U.S. only)
- **Work4Women** – Cool Jobs Same samples of non-traditional occupations. http://www.work4women.org/cooljobs/cooljobs.cfm e-mail info@work4women.org Or call 1-202-638-3143/fax 1-202-638-4885
- **Wider Opportunities for Women** – Occupations considered non-traditional. http://www.workplacesolutions.org/about/jobs2.cfm e-mail info@workplacesolutions.org

VOLUNTEERING

- **Most known diseases** have their own societies or foundations. Check on the Internet, libraries or local volunteer agencies for information.
- **Canadian Administrators of Volunteer Services** http://www.cavr.org/
- **Charity Village** (Canada) leading on-line source of information, news, jobs, services and resources for the Canadian non-profit community. http://www.charityvillage.com/
- **Goodwill Industries** – have retail stores where they help train people with barriers http://locator.goodwill.org/ Select U.S. or Canada to find a Goodwill near you.
- **Idealist** – a project of Action Without Borders lists over 46,000 non-profit and community organizations from 165 countries and thousands of volunteer opportunities. http://www.idealist.org/ Click on organizations on the right side, and then click United States or Canada. It describes each organization and contact information for each state or province.
- **United Way** helps support many non-profit organizations around the world. http://www.uwint.org/gppweb/index.aspx Click 'Where We Are' on the left, then 'North America' to find an agency near you.
- **Variety International—The Childrens's Charity** – Variety International is dedicated to improving the lives of children throughout the world. http://www.varietychildrenscharity.org/ e-mail variety.international@verizon.net
- **Volunteer Centers in Canada** http://www.volunteer.ca/index-eng.php e-mail vcs@volunteer.ca
- **Yahoo hotjobs** provides a section about volunteering http://ca.hotjobs.yahoo.com
- **Zonta International** "Advancing the status of women worldwide" http://www.zonta.org/site/PageServer e-mail zontaintl@zonta.org. or call 1-312-930-5848/fax 1-312-930-0951

About the Author

Heather Resnick

Heather is a two-time cancer warrior and lifelong learner. During her twenty years as a homemaker, she volunteered in several community projects and her children's schools. She went back to university as a mature student to get her B.A. She has personal and extensive experience with women considering re-entering the workplace.

Now following her dream of being a writer, Heather has written her first novel *Ms. Humpty Dumpty* (www.ms.humptydumpty.com). It is a "powerhouse of emotions" about a woman who constantly falls off the wall and tries to put her pieces back together again.

Heather's work has been published in magazines, newspapers and on-line. As a motivational speaker she provides practical advice using humor and her understanding of the human condition. Heather's vision is to help women become happily self-sufficient.

Could someone you know benefit from reading *Women Reworked?* It is the perfect gift—the definitive story book and resource guide.

To purchase books, e-books, reports, CD with directory or to have Heather Resnick speak:

Call   905-889-4669
Toll-free   1-800-687-2169
Fax   905-731-5189
E-mail   hrighter@rogers.com
Web site   www.womenreworked.com
Mail   1 Promenade Circle
            P.O. Box 964,
            Thornhill, ON L4J 4P0

Full name _____

Company _____

Telephone H_____ B_____ C_____

E-Mail _____

Address _____

City _____

Province/State_____

Shipping: Please add $5.00 (CAN) for first product
             + $2.00 (CAN) for each additional product
Taxes: Canadian residents, please add 7% GST

Payment:
[ ] Certified Check *or* [ ] Money Order
[ ] Credit Card: [ ] Visa   [ ] Master Card   [ ] American Express

Card Number _____

Name on card_____

Exp. Date _____

Inquire about our discounts for orders of 10 or more books.
Please allow 4-6 weeks for delivery.